Radio Controlled Model Racing Cars

D. J. Laidlaw-Dickson

Model & Allied Publications
Argus Books Ltd
14 St James Road, Watford, Herts

© L-D Editorial & Technical Services Ltd 1979
© Argus Books Ltd 1979

First published 1979

ISBN 0 84242 675 5

All rights reserved. No part of this
publication may be reproduced without
the written permission of the publishers.

Model & Allied Publications
Argus Books Ltd
14 St James Rd, Watford,
Herts, England.

Printed and bound in Great Britain by
Garrod and Lofthouse Limited,
Bedford, Bedfordshire

2

Acknowledgements

The Author acknowledges with thanks articles in this book by:
Fred Livesey
Phil Booth
Barry Tingay
Peter Crawley
Gene Husting
Paul Dudley

Notes, sketches and ideas from Racing Circuits, Chuck Hallum, Dave Martin, Ted Longshaw.

The model trade for goods provided as the background to articles and patience in discussing their products.

*The many unknowns with whom I have talked and
who have made helpful suggestions which have often
proved the source for articles.*

*Circuit drawings for the most part have been extracted from the British Radio Car Association
Handbook with the permission of the Secretary Tom Martin.*

*Front cover illustration by
Bill Burkinshaw.*

Foreword

THIS book is made up for the most part of a series of articles that have appeared in *Radio Control Model Cars,* covering all aspects of the hobby of building and racing radio controlled model cars. The greater part are my own contributions as founder/editor of the magazine, supported by a number of others and by contributors whose work is gratefully acknowledged.

With a growing interest all over the world and a fast awakening trade and technology something new is appearing nearly every few months, so that today's novelty may well be tomorrow's commonplace. The amount of information that has been available until very recently has been minimal. Now that a regular magazine is appearing progress is accelerating as ideas can be more readily exchanged and discussed. At the same time newcomers are embracing the hobby and avid for knowledge.

It would be idle to pretend that what is written here will all be valid in a year or two, but certainly it can offer the newcomer the essentials of the hobby. It tells him what it is all about, what to do, where to get the materials, where to practice the hobby or sport and put him/her right in the picture.

In the early postwar years when radio control equipment needed a large chocolate-box size container as against today's match-box size receiver, we talked of record runs following a radio controlled car in a fullsize car round some aerodrome circuit such as Silverstone to achieve time and distance records. It remained a pipe-dream for years and then some students put up a 24-hour record in Hawaii in 1975; followed this summer by two young British drivers who beat it and took the 500-mile record in addition . . . but not on Silverstone Circuit they had their own purpose built miniature race track. There are at least a dozen of them now in the country, plus many more of a less permanent nature on car parks and the like. There are others dotted all over the continent. There is a European Federation comprising some fifteen countries to organise a common racing calendar. At Monaco recently, just after the fullsize Grand Prix, the Monaco World Cup took place with the cream of the world's model drivers. An anticlimax? Not a bit of it, many spectators were heard to say, as they watched the impeccable driving of the little $\frac{1}{8}$th scale cars, that it was better than the real thing as they could see the whole of the circuit.

I hope readers will find enough in these pages to share the enthusiasm of its adherents . . . It offers many of the thrills of fullsize car racing with a fraction of the expense and none of the danger . . . plus the satisfaction of building and even designing your own potential world beater . . .

Boxmoor 1979   Dickie Laidlaw-Dickson

Contents

1 : Making a Start with Radio Control Model Cars

What It's All About

IT IS now possible for the average person — must be careful here, some of the girls are making a great show! — to build and run a radio controlled model car that will give troublefree performance and the opportunity of winning an occasional race; even sometimes surprising an expert and winning on handicap. There is no need to have any great technical skill or an elaborate workshop and tools just an urge to go out and race. In this way many people who might once have tried to storm their way into fullsize racing can enjoy all the thrills at a fraction of the cost and none of the danger.

There is a variety of kits from which to build, at prices and degrees of performance to suit all tastes; accessories are available in ever widening choice. Grand Prix, GT or simple saloon car racing is on tap; less demanding enthusiasts can settle for model Stock Car racing which is easy to set up, has limits on car cost, and has all the fun and most of the rules of the fullsize stockers. There are clubs in many parts of Britain, a number of permanent race-tracks, many others set up on a temporary basis and a national association to organise fixtures and establish acceptable racing rules. This applies to most of the world, EFRA the European controlling body has fourteen member countries; U.S.A. has ROAR (Radio Operated Automobile Racing) and there are active groups in Australia, Canada, South Africa and South America.

Tools and Accessories

The newcomer to the hobby and sport will probably already have most of the hand tools required either from earlier interest in model making or from the ordinary domestic and motor tool box. Assorted small spanners, hammer, electric soldering iron, screwdrivers make up the essential basis. A few taps and dies and a small lathe would of course be absolutely ideal but not essential.

Items that may need to be acquired are starting equipment for the internal combustion glow-plug engine in the shape of a 12 volt accumulator and a starting device. This may be a hand starter, modified slightly from those used for model aircraft (such as Sullivan or Kavan). Alternatively a fullsize car starter acquired from a car dump for a trifling sum can be rigged up to do the job splendidly. Only snag is weight and bulk — but if you have an estate car or hatchback this is no special problem. A small 2 volt accumulator is also needed to supply current to the glow plug in the engine. Some people tap their starter battery to take off 2 volt but a separate accumulator is better (Varley do a very nice one). Charging of the 12 volt would be done on the trickle charger off the mains, most car owners now have one in the garage. A neat little charger can be obtained to charge the 2 volt in the same way. A glow plug lead and connector will also be required. Finally some form of quick pourer for filling tank will be needed. But wait before getting this to see the type you fancy when you have seen other people in operation.

On the radio side you will need first of all a licence. This can be obtained in Britain from the Home Office, Radio Regulatory Department, Waterloo Bridge House, Waterloo Road, London S.E.1. This requires no test, lasts five years before renewal and costs £2.40 (U.K. only; other countries have their own similar arrangements). A radio transmitter and receiver plus a couple of servos with their appropriate batteries makes up the r/c parcel. Recharging equipment for the nicad batteries is also desirable. (Non-rechargeable batteries are right out of fashion these days). Since racing takes place against others using equipment at the same time crystal controlled equipment is a 'must'. This gives a choice of six main frequencies, differenced by colour and the user displays a coloured pennant on his transmitter aerial to show crystals in use. Two are required for each outfit, one for receiver and one for transmitter. They plug in very simply and take only a moment to change. It is possible to get additional cars going with split crystals which operate on frequencies between the main six. The keen man will have a set plus at least one split.

At the moment Futaba equipment is the popular choice both on account of its extreme reliability and because they offer a particularly robust servo capable of being abused and overloaded madly. Other makers are, however, on the ball, and there is no reason for any of a number of other makes not to be used.

Choice of Car

Cars are at the moment all of $\frac{1}{8}$ scale and come within certain specified sizes as set out elsewhere in this book.

The variety of kits is quite astonishing, but basically they all provide more or less the same group of items: a chassis base, steering (which may be partly assembled or not), wheels, tyres, back axle, flywheel and clutch, a radio plate to carry the electrical equipment (or a plastic box to house it), brake, bumperplate, sundry links and connections. A body for Grand Prix or GT may or may not be included. Some provide a made up fuel tank in metal or plastic; others provide parts and instructions for assembly.

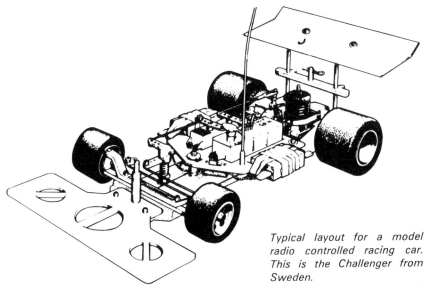

Typical layout for a model radio controlled racing car. This is the Challenger from Sweden.

7

The newcomer is strongly advised to choose a simple and fairly low priced (not necessarily the cheapest) kit and to get one that suits his style. That is if he/she is itching to get out on the track then the kit with the least work to do will be the choice. Others may like the delayed pleasure of a nice lot of making, including a fuel tank, and so get the feel of the car before actually running it. It should be said here that over the years very many ideas held until recently have been discarded, and the old adage of improvement by 'adding a little simplicity' is being rigidly followed.

If you go to a meeting or two then the variety of possibles will be seen, and an opportunity perhaps turn up to buy a second-hand car that has already been running. You will save money this way and have the added satisfaction of knowing that constructionally it will work, so that any defects in handling are your own newcomer's lack of manual dexterity rather than faults in your building.

Although a great many Grand Prix bodies and GT bodies will be seen there is nothing like so much variety underneath them. Bodies can easily be switched from one car to another so that the chassis used for GP can easily be covered by a GT body for the next event. There is no objection to this. Strangely enough, the cars go better with GT bodies than with Grand Prix as time will indicate. A third class of Saloon cars seems to be something of a Cinderella of the race track — though again a standard chassis can be used with a fresh body.

Getting to Work

Assuming that you have decided to make your car from scratch using a kit, and without too high hopes of an immediate world beater, we will try to lead you along using a couple of simple jobs as the instructions pieces. We have chosen first, a GB kit car which employs a certain number of parts from PB Products who make a series of cars from simple to sophisticated and in fact have just been scooping the National Finals meeting in a regular 'whitewash'. This car is a little up from the bottom with refinements such as ball bearings and a cast rear axle housing and one or two other goodies. The other 'guinea pig' car is an American import by Associated, foremost U.S. manufacturer, their RC2 model, which is about the simplest and lowest priced of cars. Another very modestly priced kit is the Mardave, which makes up very well. Some of our pictures illustrate points with this car.

Associated's RC2 is the starkest possible. Tyres already bonded to wheels. Plenty of useful work to do.

Mardave offer radio box, good accessories and long established reputation behind their popular low-priced kit.

The chassis base is a rectangular piece of sheet alloy, drilled in sundry places of attachment of steering and rear axle housing. This is what comes with the RC2. The GB car comes with steering unit partly assembled and in place on chassis, as is the cast rear axle housing. Building instructions vary, from the barely adequate to the excellent. Sometimes one feels with the Italians, who we note now send out their kits with no instructions at all! A tribute perhaps to the legend that every Italian has a lathe and a workshop in his back garden!

The GB kit it will be noted has a secondary platform or radio plate added to the base chassis. This enables the builder to locate his radio equipment at each side, outboard, and suspended on rubber bands to reduce the shock effects of engine vibration. Any motorcyclist knows that a single cylinder engine vibrates (as does a twin) and not until four cylinders is this overcome. Efforts to smooth out this vibration at engine level seem to make matters worse— solution is to protect the radio gear. Sight of some car racing will give the impression that the amount of dirt oil and road muck is another hazard, and surely it would be better to put the whole lot in one of the neat little plastic boxes also available. This is Mardave practice.

This is a fair point. However, in the stress and scurry of racing the problem of access arises. The plastic box has to be opened and takes non-available time, so that tendency is all towards slung radio equipment at top level. Slower racers who do not have racing crises may well prefer the box. Against this, if the engine is properly prepared, with adequate sealing of silencer attachment area, and fuel overflow is led back to spill off at the back, or to connect with silencer pot to assist in pressurising the fuel tank, then oily mess is negligible and only track dirt will come in. The air intake must also be protected against this road dirt, for, as we have heard it remarked 'it acts like a miniature vacuum cleaner sucking in every unwanted thing in the district!'

Before we get too far along with the chassis put together a word on the objects to be desired. In earlier days there was a great deal of clever springing incorporated, this has largely been discarded. What we require is a springy twisty front end which flexes and a rigid rear which does not. Hence the stout rear fitments to counteract the natural twist of the flat alloy sheet. Experts are now waisting the front end to provide even more flexion to that part. This brings up weight distribution as a factor. We want there to be plenty of weight at the back so that maximum wheel adhesion is obtained with somewhat less at the front, merely enough to provide steering. A balance point to give a 60/40% weight arrangement, or slightly more than we hope to get on the family car, is a good general allocation. This should not be too slavishly adopted at the expense of other mechanical factors.

Wheels and tyres 'as they come', before being bonded together.

For example, the shorter the connection link between servo and bellcrank, the more positive and less liable to failure it is. This has brought steering servos very much nearer the front than was formerly the case. A great deal can also be achieved in the varying hardness of tyres in providing the racing balance required. Harder at front, softer behind is the scheme, which helps to promote understeer, a desirable state, of which more anon.

Where the Engine Goes

You will not find engine mounting holes ready drilled for you in most cases, since the choice of engine is yours. Not, we must add, a very wide choice. Size will be the limit set by the rules (and as large as can conveniently be handled in $\frac{1}{8}$th scale we must add) of 3.5 cc or ranging from .19 to .21 c ins. Most popular choice and ideal for beginners is the Veco 19, which is moderately priced, easy to operate and possessed of a good tickover which is essential, together with good low speed torque. Others in use include K & B, McCoy (usually now a hybrid of Veco and McCoy — the Vecoy) Super Tigre X21 (for the experts) and more recently the moderately priced Fuji which is Schnuerle ported, but as yet untried seriously.

These in their turn all require a sophisticated carburettor, and main types in use include Perry, Kavan and the slide type exemplified by the Thorp. But to return to engine mounting. Chassis will have a rectangular hole cut in it just forward of rear axle mounting. This is to allow the flywheel to protrude slightly below the chassis bottom for starting purposes. The spur gear which comes in front of the flywheel must be located to mate with the larger gear which goes on the rear wheel and is driven by the engine. Gear ratio will vary between four and five to one, or say sixty-five teeth to twelve to fifteen teeth. A common ratio will be about 4.25/1. A well tuned top class car may well be running at 25,000 to 30,000 rpm and attaining **real** (ie NOT scale) speeds of up to 70 mph! But not while you're still a beginner please.

Set up the rear wheels, mount the flywheel and clutch on the engine and offer it to the larger spur gear for good mesh. Not a binding mesh but a neat approach. A good way to judge it is to put a couple of thicknesses of cigarette paper between the two gears — this gives just about the right amount of clearance. Mark carefully where this locates the engine. A friend with a helping hand is useful here.

With the RC2 kit two useful engine mounts are provided and have a slotted hole in each to allow for some slight forward/backward movement but not sideways. Engine is screwed onto these and two main holes popped and drilled out $\frac{3}{16}$ in dia in the chassis plate, so that the flywheel comes evenly through the ready made hole with space all round and meshing nicely — it may therefore not necessarily be laterally central in the hole but with clearance.

Fitting the Clutch

This is stepping back in assembly sequence and would be done before installing engine of chassis. Clutches vary in detail but are the same in principle. Two clutch shoes are each attached at a single point and can pivot on that point like a couple of railway signals. As the engine revs up these shoes are spun out by centrifugal force and come up against the round inner surface of a bellhousing which fits over them, and, taking a grip on this, spin the driving wheels. It is a constant matter of surprise to me that this actually works! It does, and is exactly the same as I was fitting to model cable racing cars some thirty years ago, so it has had quite a long testing time. The shoes are held in place by little springs which the speeding-up motor overcomes as the throttle is opened. The inside of the bellhousing is lined with similar material to that used for brake linings to give a suitable amount of bite and grip. Some shoes are of metal, others of such materials as tufnol. In some cases the holding-in springs are dispensed with and the shoes act without restraint. Until revs of the motor build up the car will idle without creeping forward on the ground. Adjusting the holding back springs will bring forward motion sooner or later as desired, but a degree of clutch slip makes for a more manageable car. **A word of warning!** Some of the parts for a clutch to be assembled (notably Associated's) are very small so put them together over a sheet of white paper, keeping bits not in use in an envelope or small tin. Alternatively, do as I did, and order a spare set of mini bits thus avoiding crawling over the floor looking for tiny dropped items.

Right: Ubiquitous Veco 19 with Kavan carburettor and Mardave silencer.

Below: Simple radio plate, solid back axle fittings with ballbearings are features of the GB kit.

Typical clutch components. Note stout spring on two shoes and clutch bell lining.

Up to the Front

Now to get the steering end sorted. The GB car has its steering in place already and only needs to be touched up with a file to round off any rough edges that are sure to catch you sooner or later. Associated RC2 needs to be made up. Nearly all nuts are locknuts and need quite a bit of effort screwing home, so that a good box spanner or two is desirable. I usually put a head in the bench vice where layout makes this possible and screw up with the box spanner. The two long nuts holding steering wishbones will also double as holding pieces for the body at a later stage in construction.

In the more expensive and sophisticated kits many parts here are moulded but with 'cooking' kits the kingpin assemblies and pivot arms must be screwed up with the stub axles to make up into left and right hand units. Pivot arms may be pieces of twisted metal or angle with suitable holes drilled in them to take track rods later. Sometimes they will align the wheels straight ahead or may be bent to give an Akerman effect. That is to say if they were extended they should meet just ahead of the rear axle. Ideally, the inside wheel on a turn will describe a smaller circle than the outside wheel otherwise there must be a certain amount of scrub with the inner wheel doing less than its share of work. Some drivers will claim that since the inner wheel tends to lift on a corner anyway it does not really matter. However, the more expert will be delighted with the ingenious linkage recently developed by PB Products which does indeed give the proper theoretical response on a turn.

We are concerned with the more mundane toe-in. Wheels should be adjusted slightly 'pigeon-toed' up to about 15 degrees in all, that is $7\frac{1}{2}$ degrees for each wheel. This improves steering and directional stability — full size drivers will also say it is hard on the tyres but this is an area where the model must exaggerate to obtain its effect. This adjustment is achieved by means of the track rod joining the two steering pivot arms. This track rod is a simple length of 16 swg piano wire, clipped into the holes provided either by bending up the wire and fitting a washer over the end, or with special spring clips. It is usual to have one end of the track rod threaded to enable adjustments to be made quickly when testing. A little additional length to enable a V bend to be added to the track rod also provides this facility and is a form of servo saver.

This brings up the next little matter. If and when the car meets an obstacle it may be prevented by its bulk or location from completing the manoeuvre that has been signalled to it. The servo still goes on trying to do the necessary but in vain. It may overheat and be ruined in consequence. The servo saver or overrider a form of spring loaded bellcrank takes care of this. Other devices are in use to achieve the same end. The American RC-2 has springs in little tubes which perform the same task. Once again PB Products have their own special gimmick which looks after this and provides excellent steering properties.

So far we have linked our wheels with a track rod and set up their toe-in. Another shorter length of piano wire is needed to come from the bellcrank/servo saver to one of the steering arms and connect via another of the holes drilled in it. It does not matter which side you attach, object is to have the shortest possible linkage from servo through to action station, wherever it may be. Once again we meet the option, whether to have servos tucked away neatly in a radio crate or out in the open as near the action as may be. This latter tactic is the one mostly followed though it means leaving the security of the radio plate and coming right up close to the steering.

Stop and Go

With the chassis now beginning to look fuller and more like business we go back to the engine end. According to the kit in hand the rear axle may have plain bearings on angle brackets, be fitted with ball races and have a solid cast bearing plate. We have fitted our engine, checked the clutch and seen the gears engaging properly. The servo which operates the speed control on the engine, paradoxically also works the brake. When it is pushed in one direction it opens throttle, then comes back at midway point to engine tickover, but on being pulled the other way brings a very simple brake into operation. So simple is it indeed that you may wonder if it really works. It does.

A half or less circle of curved sheet metal to which is stuck a layer of cork or rubber is pressed against the flywheel and rapidly checks forward motion. In some cases the lining is omitted and there is just the contact of brass sheet against iron flywheel. Since the clutch is centrifugal and only accepts the engine thrust at some fairly high rate of revs this action is comparatively gentle but really does bring results. Just as at the steering end there was a servo saver, here again an over ride or spring loaded device is fitted, though probably not quite so essential here.

Steering detail on Mardave. Note failsave linkage and kink in track rod for fine adjustment of toe-in.

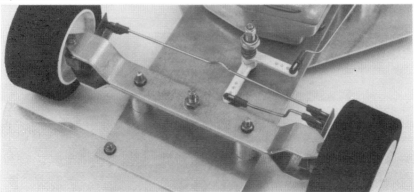

Left: Dustbin silencer, 'big head' heat sink, carburettor filter and springloaded servo saver linkage to disc brake.

Opposite, below: A similar set-up showing fuel tank with overflow leading back into dustbin silencer 'rat race' type filler cap and radio gear elastic slung between pillars, which also serve to locate body.

In one or two cases kits on offer have the brake drum as a separate item from the clutch, located on the back axle inboard from the axle bearings. This obviously relieves pressure on the flywheel that just conceivably might increase engine wear, but usually there is so much at that end of the car that space is not readily available. It is also possible to fit disc brakes, but this is stepping right into the experts' class and need not be considered at least for a few races.

Two things remain to be done engine wise. Connection between fuel tank and engine must be broken by the insertion of a fuel filter. This can be unscrewed and after a race or two the muck it catches will convince a doubting Thomas of its value. Similarly the air intake requires a filter for dirt can so easily be sucked in there. Foam devices are available and quite sophisticated honeycomb devices or a simple fine mesh gauze can be wired over. It must not be open meshed enough to let grit pass or so fine that not even enough air is let in.

Tanks

What sort of fuel tank should we be using? At the very bottom of the tree we can fit one of those simple translucent plastic tanks primarily used for model boat running. This offers a simple container with connection to a fuel line to the engine and a suitable opening with press on or screw top cap. Capacity will be something under the 4 oz permitted racing size. There is nothing wrong with this, fitting should follow any building instructions given, so that location does not bring supply into a flooding position with the engine, that is not above carburettor level. Attachment to the chassis or radio plate will be by rubber bands to reduce risk of foaming by vibration, though this is unlikely to happen.

If we decide to be more ambitious we can follow the GB Models solution, which provides a shiny tin and lid (perhaps from the same place as the Coleman mustard tins come?) two short bits of metal tube, $\frac{1}{4}$ and $\frac{1}{2}$ in dia to be fitted, and a couple of longer lengths of thinner brass tube to provide feed and ventilation in the tank. You, the operator, will be expected to find a discarded metal tin lid off an empty $\frac{1}{2}$-pint fuel can or similar to complete the metalwork. Final need is the fuel cap, which should permit easy no-time-at-all filling and yet hold in the fuel, in other words a 'rat race' cap from the model aero world. Putting this together is a splendid exercise in soldering, even if in disgust you throw the whole thing away afterwards! I did! And started again to do it more elegantly. If you have not been soldering much recently you do tend to lose the knack, but it comes back, and an untidy job is an abomination.

The two things to remember in soldering are hot iron, repeat HOT IRON, and clean tinned surfaces. Then you cannot go wrong it is a matter of tidy manual dexterity with the tool, you do not need a lot of solder, a little in the right place is far far better. If you find it a bit too much at the moment, forget it, and acquire a ready-made metal tank. The tank we have just described is known as a 'chicken hopper' tank enabling the last drop of fuel to be used, rather than slopping about in the bottom of a large flat area it all goes down into that little rescued tin lid. A completely made-up version can be obtained.

Other sophisticated tank versions are also on the market, including pressurised tanks where fuel line vent is lead back into silencer pot to increase pressure.

Whatever tank you decide upon connection to engine must be via fuel tubing, clear plastic tubing sold for the job. It will fit in a tight push fit over the tank lead out pipe and on to the engine fuel intake.

Silencer

In these days of noise abatement regulations good neighbour relations make good silencing of engines imperative. BRCA regulations require that noise level is kept to official limit of 80dB at 10 metres. Such a level is not difficult to attain and a number of commercial silencers are available. They vary from the small simple Mardave type (in two varieties for racing and stock cars — so be sure to get the sort you need — the exhaust pipe comes out at a different angle) which is recommended for the beginner. Being small it offers few attachment problems and whilst it may not be so efficient as the larger 'dust-bin' type silencers this slight efficiency drop is not really to be deplored for the beginner.

Attachment method will vary with make (and even model) of engine. Veco can be attached via a dumb-bell like fixing that goes through holes in the exhaust opening and then has a single screw fixing. Other Veco castings lack these holes, so that an all-round strap fitting is needed. Most other silencers are fitted with this sort of strap. The 'dustbin' silencer usually sits upright on a small chassis extension at the rear, and has an additional metal fitting to clamp on to engine opening, the whole being joined with a short length of large diameter plastic tubing. There is also a large 'dustbin' type that straps round like its smaller versions.

Heatsink

Unlike model aircraft where the engine enjoys cooling breezes the car engine is tucked away and tends to get very hot. A heatsink is therefore essential to carry away this overheating. This may be a flat ribbed plate which slips on to the cylinder head or of a more fancy shape. Super Tigre X21 includes one with the engine, but this is not usual. Just recently a number of 'big heads' have been on offer which take the place of the standard cylinder head for cooling purposes. These are certainly more attractive and it is indeed a 'cosmetic' solution. However, the keen but impecunious builder can very well make up his own from scrap alloy. Take a look at those you can see and you will realise how simple they are to make at a fraction of the cost.

2: The Great Electric Car Explosion

DECLINE OF slot-car racing left Japanese manufacturers with a considerable capacity and little market so that it is not surprising their thoughts turned elsewhere. Free flight electric powered aircraft came along which was a great help, and then suddenly there appeared on the British market the Cyclone and Bullet electric motors, direct descendants of the slot car specials. The same motors have appeared all over the modelling world under a variety of 'badge names' but are very much the same thing. In U.S.A. they were seized upon eagerly as power units for a new generation of free-running electric powered r/c controlled model cars — the long sought ideal was here at last!

This all happened several years ago, long enough for our American friends to have got commercially organised and to have formulated appropriate classes in their racing associaticns. It only hit the British market in 1977 with the advent of the Lectricar. This is (apart from the Japanese motor!) a strictly British enterprise that has been enjoying a startling and well-merited success.

But what is this electric r/c model car racing? We nearly all have encountered the simple single channelled little $\frac{1}{16}$th scale cars that have a left oriented turn and come complete with transmitter at what is today's pocket-money price. These are great fun

Below: Scene at an inter-club meeting at Leamington held in part of the outdoor (nearly) showroom of the local Ford dealers Soan's. Two level floor provided a natural rostrum for drivers.

Above left: Lectricar front axle beam and failsafe. Above right: Original Lectricar speed control and charging leads inserted.

but obviously of limited interest to the 'enthusiast' operator. The standard car on offer as a kit uses the smaller Cyclone motor powered by six rechargeable nicads producing a total of 7.2 volts. Speed control is by microswitches that provide three forward and three reverse speeds operated by servo; a second servo takes care of the steering.

The kit itself is offered as a simple assembly project, and is indeed just this. Full marks for a beautifully prepared box of parts where everything really fits billing. Scale is 1/12th with choice at the moment of two bodies from the manufacturers — Ford Escort or Porsche. These are simple ABS plastics which require windows to be cut out and a paint job done but are adequate for the job.

Steering has an adequate failsafe servo saver; a neat plastic radio box is provided and servos can be mounted with double-sided tape without much fear of motor vibration from the electrics doing them any harm. A single charge of the motor will provide up to ten minutes running time. This is achieved via the charging leads provided which can be clipped onto the terminals of the family car battery to provide the current. Maximum length of charge should not exceed twenty minutes which gives approximately half that time running. More usually users will acquire their own 12-volt battery/accumulator which may be any reasonably portable type. Trend is towards the lighter weight motor cycle battery of which the excellent Varley 12. 7/10 20 hour is a good example. Less expensive and less powerful is the WB 12/T5 but adequate for electric recharging (whether it is man enough to run a starter for i.c. powered cars has yet to be discovered). When buying a battery be sure to get it filled with acid — often they are described as 'dry charged' which means what it says. Acid is cheap but regulations on sale make it impossible to buy a bottle to take away.

Left: Bo-Link (USA) use a wiper type rheostat for speed control. Below: Mardave steering and failsafe on their prototype.

Meanwhile, in Britain at least one other manufacturer, Mardave, is tooling up and should be releasing their variety of electric car as this appears. Indeed, only full order books for their ⅛th scale racing and stockcar kits have kept them back until now. Wes Rayner of Mardave is following a very different line by miniaturising to 1/12 scale the standard ⅛th scale layout, with the batteries (six nicad cells) slung outboard, where in fullsize GP racing cars it is customary to locate the petrol tanks. In addition the Mardave car will operate with proportional speed control rather than the microswitch sequence, which should make for much smoother running and absence of twitchiness. Proper speed control is obviously the way to do it, though initial cost and the heat engendered, provide problems for the manufacturer.

A limited number of American made cars and kits are coming in; adverse exchange rates make them fairly expensive, but there is no doubt of their quality and the advantage they have enjoyed of being on the market now for some time. A good variety of tyres in a range of hardnesses, specifically for indoor or outdoor use is most valuable. A complete ready to run car with 'street' Porsche body and driver is available. Other options include receiver-servo 'bricks' which are installed and require only a transmitter to get moving, that is motor / receiver / servos / control are in the one unit. Then a version of this offers a 'power train' which gives chassis, motor, speed control, axles, steering as a package. Wheels, servos, radio, body are extra. Quite a wide range of 1/12th scale bodies in clear Lexan are on the market. These have also been prepared for the smaller 1/12th scale i.c. range popular in U.S.A. and so is more extensive than could, at present, be expected from an electric car market alone.

Where can electric cars be run? Virtually any drill hall, church hall, gymnasium, or even a decent sized patio at home can be used. There is no oily deposit, no smell, and a very low noise factor so that a meeting should be welcomed by even the most pernickety Vicar or school caretaker. A number of very successful free-for-all evenings have been held already in the Palm Court of Alexandra Palace, in North London. This hall is used normally for roller skating and tends to be highly polished — not ideal for cars — but the management have been co-operative in cleaning it down to improve road-holding.

Reasonable limit for an evening's racing is thirty-two cars. This allows for the usual six frequencies to be employed plus two split frequencies, to give eight cars to a race. A five minute race allows some practice lappery in the ten minutes full charge. As each

Below: One of the many Mardave versions produced prior to release of their car.

Above: Bo-Link Porsche kit, showing body, nicad cells, rehostat, steering arrangement and charging leads.

entrant completes his race he can then put his name and frequency colour down for the next free slot (rather like club tennis!) With luck everyone can get in a minimum of three runs an evening, or perhaps a little more over a three-hour period. A small fee is charged to drivers to cover hall hire.

With the present forward/reverse only minimal marshalling is needed as cars can reverse away from hazards — usually wheelbarrow tyres at the corners. Circuit layout is established with simple stick down adhesive plastic tapes, or can be chalked on. A decent long straight plus two or three dog legs to establish changes of lock can soon total up to an interesting lap length of a hundred yards in quite modestly sized halls. Driver should stand a little off the ground — beer (or even milk) crates are ideal for this.

So far racing has taken place under the auspices of the British Radio Car Association who have provided organisation and lap scoring facilities in London (notably Messrs. Dave Rogers, Brian Field, Ellis) and arranged Ally Pally hire. Regulations have been minimal; only that motor is Cyclone (or identical 'badge' named motor) and nicads do not exceed six in number, ie, norminal 7.2v.) Division into GP and GT classes may become desirable when other car choices more generally available. We look to hear of many more electric car meetings throughout Britain during the winter months.

3: British Electrics

AFTER NEARLY a year's solo run, Lectricar have been joined in the electric rc model car market by Mardave offering a completely different approach to the subject. When Dave Bailey and Steve Talbot joined forces to manufacture the Lectricar they decided to produce a unit that could not be faulted for quality with price — in a field then unestablished — as a secondary consideration. This search for perfection extended even to the large round head screws used, all made in the factory. Wes Raynor tackled the problem from a strictly Mardave angle. Mardave have been making their racing cars and stock cars from the establishment of the hobby in this country at rock bottom prices, and this was the course to be followed with the new product.

In this the company has succeeded magnificently with a kit retailing at around £37.50, complete with body, motor, all necessary parts, nicads, requiring only servos and r/c gear to complete. The same specification, of course, is followed by Lectricar though at an appreciably higher price. Let us be quite firm, however, on this matter of price, frankly I don't know how Mardave do it! I accept that the Lectricar price is also remarkably low for the quality of the product. Coming in later Mardave may have had the advantage of bypassing some production problems that cost money, but they always intended to have a price 'under £40'. The two rival kits will doubtless continue side by side, the lighter Mardave with slightly less purpose-built parts, and the benefit of larger

Below: The Mardave electric car. Speed control is exposed below wing. This car also uses non-standard alloy wheels and inserts.

Above left: Mardave side-slung nicads help weight distribution. Above right: Lectricar steering with forward body mount for the Porsche body.

Mardave cars to effect economies in material purchases, plus the opportunity to use up a higher proportion of the sheet rubber out of which tyres are stamped. For racing enthusiasts this lighter weight may account for their present run of success at meetings (without detracting anything from drivers' skill, please).

The Kits Side by Side

This is very much a personal preference game, but we can look at the two kits and consider in what ways they differ. Lectricar started with a fairly expensive microswitch speed control system which was not entirely satisfactory on highly polished floors, as racers at Alexandra Palace and elsewhere soon found out, though excellent for rough wood or school playground surfaces. The switch to a printed circuit panel to provide proportional control was a logical move. This type of control which is really an improved form of rheostat control still generates heat, but not all that much now that special heat sink types of printed circuit board have become available. Mardave from the start has been developed with printed panel proportional control in mind as a simple, relatively inexpensive method. The expensive transistorised 'black boxes' on offer are the ultimate answer but costly, and require near duplication of parts to provide reverse.

Throughout 1976 the Mardave test team has been running cars with minor variation after variation to get the simplest possible reliable control. All the usual problems of overload and burning out of panels by sparking have been encountered and cured. A truly frustrating period this must have been for Wes, with thousands of motors and

Below left: Lectricar modified speed control; note also new rear bumper. Below right: Mardave speed control with servo built into plate (linkages not fitted for clarity).

stacks of parts all ready to go, but held back until he was quite certain it was as near foolproof as it could be.

First major difference between the kits is the location of the nicads. Lectricar put theirs in a neat stack, boxed and unobtrusive in the rear centre of the chassis base plate. Round them goes the U-shaped box holding the radio gear. Mardave preferred to put theirs in two sausage strings, one each side of the chassis length, where on a fullsize car the petrol tanks would go. Less neat and tidy, but theoretically the better place for weight distribution. It also encourages use of a low slung body with cells lying flat instead of upright.

Steering systems also differ. Lectricar have the clever springloaded tong system, first seen on model cars in America. Mardave have adopted a smaller version of that used on some of their stock cars, with straight in-line springing, which probably achieves some production saving. The early Lectricars had a slight design fault in that cars could be rammed from the rear to damage the control plate. This is now altered with a stout alloy plate bent up to protect this vulnerable part. Mardave have theirs poised well over the engine mounting and out of harm's way. In their instructions (mine are original first 200 test run words) it is necessary to cut into the plastic plate holding the control panel to take the steering servo. This is perhaps a pity if several cars are being run from time to time and only limited servos available. I have just seen a Greeno treatment that appeals, where servo is not so attached. The plastic bracket for aerial webbing and holding receiver on/off switch is slightly cut away to allow servo (Futaba 16) to stand upright. Usual largish Futaba nicad is not used, but the smaller half power job (as offered by several other manufacturers) which is almost square only takes half the space and so permits this.

Lectricar have now added a Porsche 936 to their range of bodies (Ford Escort, Porsche 'Street') and provide hexagonal pillar fixing like the 'big' model car. Mardave delight me by using Velcro tape for attaching bodies. I am now using it extensively from

Below: A new British kit the Spectron in prototype form. Skyleader radio equipment is fitted together with Smoothtronic proportional controls that eliminate radio battery and speed control servo.

Left: A nice colour scheme in blue and white for the Mardave body, painted by Steve Busby.

fixing loose covers to the furniture at home to sensible model uses like this. It is quite secure enough for use in this scale if a bit hazardous with ⅛th (but we shall see).

Mardave have the pretty Turbo Porsche 935 body as their saloon offering, and the less popular BRM Formula body. I have also just seen a couple of other non-standard bodies that can be fitted, and a modification to convert to a six-wheel Tyrrell. There will be a spate of bodies for both kits in the months to come.

The Coming Craze

Dan Rutherford in a lead article of this title in the U.S. magazine *Model Retailer* tells of the beginning of an Electric R/C Car Pay Circuit, where you buy time and use the 'house' cars and radio equipment. It is sophisticated enough and stout enough for this to be possible even with unskilled operators! Run in conjunction with a model shop it not only pays its way as a track, but also promotes additional shop sales. This is encouraging in one way: alarming in another. As the author points out, no American trader can see this prospect without harking back to the slot-car pay tracks of the sixties and the collapse of that market. This was due as much as anything 'to enthusiasts buying up the goodies' to quote the author, 'just to keep competitive, plus not being farsighted enough to realise that they were fast getting to the point where nobody could afford to compete'. This same thing killed cable racing in the U.K., when speed enough to win was too dear to buy.

The answer must be in the hands of national race sanctioning bodies, perhaps by arranging appropriate groups to give all classes of drivers and equipment a fair crack of the whip. This looks like the present pattern as developing with electrics . . . let us all be careful not to fall into the trap of 'I can **afford** a faster car than thou'!

Right: Lectricar Porsche bodied. Front bumper enlarged, side fixing studs re-arranged to stay pointing outwards, and studs holding radio box re-located to take servos more conveniently.

4: Tuning Mysteries

Fred Livesey

The author is an engineering instructor at a government skill centre where emphasis rests on results not theory so is specially qualified to give practical tips.

FIRST LET me say that the title of this piece probably sums up the average modellers attitude towards 'Tuning'.

Then let me say that 'Mystery' and 'Magic' are not the secrets of a successfully tuned engine.

I believe that a well known racing engine designer has said that the success of his Formula 1 engine lies in the fact that he went back to basics.

Before we discuss the basics perhaps a few observations are required on highly developed engines. To win a race — you must finish — a fact that we all too often tend to forget. Reliability must therefore be our first Consideration. Cars which finish only 8 laps (albeit in half the time of the others) don't take homelaurels — I know from experience.

A further observation concerns the development of the full size racing two-stroke engines. Modifications which make a Suzuki or a Yamaha so much faster do not necessarily work on our small engines. Unless of course you find a way of making ⅛th scale fuel particles. Furthermore full-size engines usually use 10 speed gearboxes and rev. to 25,000 RPM — we use single speed and I believe ('though this may cause some controversy) rev. at 40,000 RPM. — under load. This fact probably accounts for the engine bearing casualties at the Nationals this year. Bearing manufacturers rev. limits on the sizes we use, with a riveted cage, are 25,000 RPM. HELP! First reliability problems which as yet cannot be overcome.

Back to the basics. There are distinct areas where improvements can be attained with time and patience.

The time and patience are required to carry out the modifications and test, re-test, and even more testing to prove that there is in fact an improvement. The improvements can be considered under separate headings as follows:

1. Reliability — the most important.
2. Mechanical efficiency — to reduce friction within the engine.
3. Volumetric efficiency — the filling of the cylinder with the maximum quantity of fresh combustible mixture possible.
4. Combustion efficiency — the amount of potential heat available from the fuel mixture which is turned into actual heat.
5. Thermal efficiency — Amount of heat (from 4) converted into mechanical energy.
6. Increasing the number of power strokes per minute — ie, RPM.

Most of the engines we use are mass produced with varying tolerances — hence the occasions when one engine straight from the box goes like hell, and yet another appears to be down on power. By carefully checking our engines we can get quite useful gains of power. This is known in full-size racing circles as 'Blueprinting'.

Before going on lets look at the equipment required:

1. Electric drill on bench stand.
2. Various lengths and diameters of wooden dowel.
3. Degree disc and pointer. (Two protractors glued to white cardboard — fits on crankshaft. Pointer — $\frac{1}{16}$ welding rod — fits on cylinder head screw).
4. Shim steel — various.
5. High speed grinding tool (Dremel Precision Petite or flexible shaft on drill).
6. Various small grinding stones and burrs.
7. Old pan for hot water, scrubbing brushes, soap and metal polish.
8. Stop watch for testing.
9. A luxury really — Testing dynamometer brake — saves time on testing.

Let's now look at each section in turn.

Reliability, as previously stated, must be our first priority when considering improvements. Whilst discussing each section any problems which could affect this will be pointed out.

Mechanical efficiency, can be improved on all mass produced engines and one could say that it is 'something for nothing'. Friction is the main cause of reduced mechanical efficiency. Piston and con-rod mis-alignment, and incorrect piston to cylinder running clearances generate the greatest amounts of friction. Simple checking jigs can be constructed to check con-rod alignment (see Fig 1) and piston and con-rod alignment (see Fig 2).

Piston to liner fit unfortunately can only be decided by experiment to strike a happy medium between good sealing and the minimum amount of friction. To check for fit immerse both parts in almost boiling water. The piston should feel stiff when pushed through cylinder without lubrication, but should slide easily when lubricated. The method I use to ease tight pistons is to lap piston to cylinder with metal polish up to a point $\frac{1}{8}$ in from cylinder head face (see Fig 3). Thoroughly wash piston and liner in hot

Figs 1 and 2 Con rod alignment jig and piston to gudgeon pin alignment.

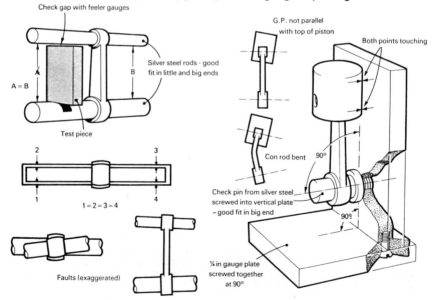

26

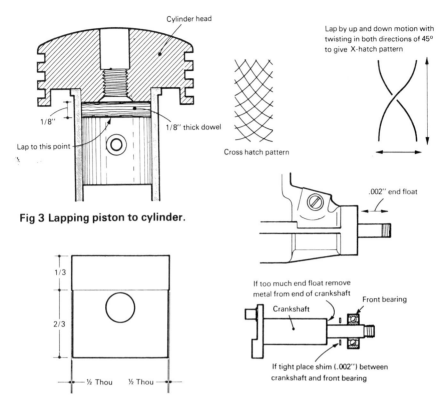

Fig 3 Lapping piston to cylinder.

Fig 4 Skirt relieving on piston.

Fig 5 Camshaft end float.

soapy water before each check. This gives excellent sealing on initial combustion and also relieves friction. Another method which has already been carried out by some engine manufacturers is to reduce the piston skirt diameter by .001 (see Fig 4). ($\frac{1}{2}$ thou each side).

This can be carried out by carving a piece of dowel to be a tight push fit up the inside of the piston and placing the dowel in an electric drill on a bench stand. By using 400 grade wet and dry abrasive paper with paraffin the piston skirt is easily relieved.

Another cause of friction which is often overlooked is that caused by distortion of the cylinder liner when hot. The distortion is caused by the port cutouts and the uneven thickness of the outer cylinder casting. To relieve this distortion it is necessary to lightly lap the cylinder liner to cylinder casting with metal polish, after heating them both in almost boiling water until an easy push fit is achieved. This is slightly difficult but it can be done if a length of wooden dowel is inserted in the cylinder liner and the crank case is held in a gloved hand.

The fit of the big end bearing should not be too tight. A slightly perceptible amount of up and down movement is required.

Ball bearings in the engine should be checked for tightness or roughness. There should be at least .002 end float in the crankshaft to allow for crankcase expansion when hot (see Fig 5). Use the aforementioned hot water method to check.

This about wraps up the friction side of things and can alone give quite useful gains.

The volumetric efficiency — though sounding complicated is really quite simple. It is the greatest amount of fresh combustible charge with which the cylinder can be filled — or — the breathing of the engine.

The list of items which improve the breathing are:
1. The length of the induction period.
2. The inlet, transfer and exhaust port areas.
3. The shape of transfer passages.
4. The crankcase capacity or pumping efficiency.
5. A minimum of restrictions in the exhaust.
6. The temperature of the incoming charge.

Plenty of areas for improvement when you think that each complete cycle or two revolutions of the engine takes only three thousandths of a second at 40,000 rpm.

The carburettor bore is the first restriction which must be checked, but this must not be overdone or the bottom-end power of the engine may be reduced. A bore of 9/32 in seems to give a reasonable compromise. Again, this is a feature which only testing can really decide, by starting at $\frac{1}{4}$ in and testing with gradual increases until the conditions that provide good bottom-end power without any restrictions in top-end performance prevail.

The type of induction porting used by most of the engines in model cars is of the front induction variety. We have to modify the crankshaft to ensure that (a) the port is pen long enough and (b) the passage is not obstructed.

In (a) only testing can show the modifications that are required. Before carrying out an modifications the timing of the crankshaft port should be checked with a degree disc and pointer.

Turn engine to top dead centre (TDC), adjust degree disc with pointer at zero. Check reading at bottom dead centre (BDC). Turning engine in the direction of rotation note reading as intake port opens after BDC. This should be in the 30 degree to 40 degree region. Continue turning engine, check at the point the inlet port closes — from 40 degrees to 60 degrees approximately — depending on the make of engine.

As previously stated the modifications necessary can only be done on a 'suck it and see' basis. First modifying the opening period by turning the degree disc so that the port opens $2\frac{1}{2}$ degrees earlier and marking the crankshaft with a scriber.

The crankshaft is then removed and the excess metal ground back to the line.

Then, by testing, an improvement should be noticed in the bottom end performance.

Tread warily — only $2\frac{1}{2}$ degree steps. Metal can be removed but not replaced. A wise precaution is to have a spare crankshaft and record the results of the tests at the point where the performance is impaired. Go back $2\frac{1}{2}$ degrees, and this is the port opening period which gives best results. A similar operation will have to be carried out on the closing point of the port.

This is where the patience comes in — but you can't get 'owt for nowt' at this stage of tuning. The port shape and crankshaft bore can be modified — (see FIg 6). Transfer passage shape should be as large as possible at the crankcase end, tapering to the same size as the ports in the cylinder liner with minimum steps and venturic shape (see Fig 7). Transfer and exhaust port timing can be increased in a similar manner to inlet port, but again, tread warily.

The crankcase capacity is one area in which improvements have yet to be tested. However, an interesting fact is that a reduction in capacity ie, rear disc induction, only improves top end performance, and for our application we still need a reasonable bottom end performance. This has to do with the fact that if the speed of the transfer is

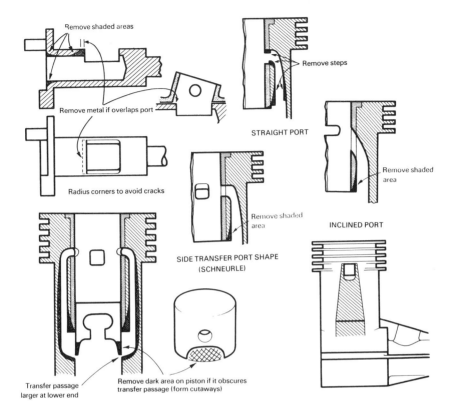

Fig 6 Crankshaft modifications.   Fig 7 Port and transfer passage shapes.

increased, too much mixing of fresh charge with the exhaust gases takes place. This cannot be avoided altogether in the two stroke engine.

The exhaust system should be designed to avoid the above phenomena — and figures indicate that if the silencer is made ten times the cylinder capacity, the minimum amount of back pressure is present. Tuned pipes are of use only at one particular crankshaft speed and limit the power at other speeds. Ideal for planes and boats running at maximum revs, but not for model cars. I may be proved wrong in the future — but we'll see.

Temperature of incoming charge is an area where little has been done. As the mixture is heated it expands — crankcase cooling is a possibility here: Combustion efficiency depends on the fuel used, turbulence in, and temperature of the cylinder head — and glow plugs.

Fuel used is a mixture of methanol, nitromethane, and lubricating oil. The percentage of lubricating oil reduces the amount of combustible fuel in the charge, so the minimum amount of oil that canbe used without affecting reliability increases combustion efficiency.

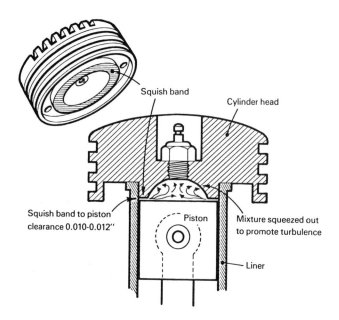

Fig 8 Squish band.

percentage of lubricating oil reduces the amount of combustible fuel in the charge, so the minimum amount of oil that can be used without affecting reliability increases combustion efficiency.

The nitromethane content has a direct bearing on combustion efficiency. Nitromethane is a fuel additive which is rich in oxygen when burned with methanol. The more oxygen available during combustion the better.

Percentages of nitromethane in the fuel mixture have been the cause of some controversy in the past, but the correct method is to increase the percentage slowly from about 15% until no noticeable increase in power is found. With a high nitro content the fuel tends to see off glow plugs rapidly (I heard a story of 20 plugs used at one meeting) — so beware! Also, nitro is now very expensive — and with 5% an improvement in tick over will be found.

Turbulence in the cylinder head is caused by the squish band area (see Fig 8). When discussing thermal efficiency we'll look at this. Temperature in the cylinder head should be around 80degC. I use the rule of thumb method of spitting in the head — if it sizzles it's about right — try various heat sinks.

Glow plugs vary between manufacturers, and even between the same type. Unfortunately this is one area we can do little other than find one type that with our particular engine gives maximum power and reliability.

Thermal efficiency is tied up with combustion efficiency in many ways. All the mixture in the combustion chamber must be burned to the best advantage.

The compression ratio of the engine has a direct bearing on thermal efficiency. With the fuel we use, very high compression ratios are possible. The only limiting factor at the moment is the glow plug elements. The difference betweeeen actual and swept volume compression ratios on our engines is the fact that the actual ratio is measured from the point the exhaust port closes. The swept volume is for the full 3.5 cc capacity, ie, full stroke. For ease of calculation we will use swept volume. The ratio needed is between 10-12 to 1 — again see which gives best performance.

The formula for checking compression ratio is:

$$CR = \frac{\text{Swept volume of cylinder} + \text{volume of combustion chamber}}{\text{Volume of combustion chamber}}$$

These can be checked by making plugs of plasticine in the shape of the swept cylinder and the combustion chamber. By using a measuring glass $\frac{1}{2}$-full of water the amount displaced when the plasticine is immersed is the size of each. Using the above formula work out the compression ratio.

Turbulence aids thermal efficiency and improves combustion efficiency. The more turbulence — the smoother the flame travels during combustion, thus giving improved power flow. The squish band aids this turbulence. Clearance between the squish band and piston which appears to give best results is .010 in to .012 in (see Fig 8).

Glow plugs also have a bearing on thermal efficiency and the matters discussed in the previous section apply.

From the foregoing comments you can see that there are many areas which can effect improvements.

5: Tuning and Bullet Proofing the Veco 19

TO APPLY the previous piece ie 'Tuning Mysteries' to specific engines seems a logical step. As there are probably more Veco 19 engines available, new and s/hand and the Veco is probably the best engine to use when learning to 'drive' model cars — this seems the best engine to begin with.

Various articles about Veco 19s have been written from time to time by different model car contributors to other magazines but as this publication is directed to model car enthusiasts exclusively then perhaps it would be better to start with the basics.

First I should say that if someone is just starting with a model car and is about to buy an engine, then a great deal of thought should be given to the purchase of a later type of schnurle ported engine. They definitely give more power, and the cost of a new Veco and the modification bits and pieces will come to more than buying a complete schnurle type engine ie: KB3.5 cc, OPS3.5 cc, STX21 etc. The advantage of a modified Veco is that the cost of repair when it becomes worn (if the chromed liner is not damaged) is the price of a new ring about £1.50 to £2.00. The cost of repairing a Schnurle with A.B.C. (Aluminium Piston in a Bronze Liner which has been Chromed will be about £8.00-£12.00). So for the beginner the Veco seems the best engine to start with, especially if a sound second engine can be bought and the McCoy modifications fitted.

Let us now consider the modifications as in my previous piece. ie.
1. Reliability.
2. Mechanical efficiency.
3. Volumetric efficiency.
4. Combustion efficiency.
5. Thermal efficiency.
6. Increasing RPM.

1. Reliability: The standard liner fitted with a cast iron piston will last about 1 to 4 hours normally, there are always exceptions to the rule and I have heard of very occasional engines which have lasted a great deal longer.

The view I take is that a much more efficient air filter fitted to the carb. than we have used over the previous years would help, but it is only now that competitors wearing out expensive ABC pistons and liners that more thought is being given to air cleaners. Not before time!

By far the best method of improving the life of a piston-liner assembly is to fit a McCoy Modification as imported by 'Irvine Engines' and Ted Longshaw'. The modification consists of a strengthened connecting rod, with larger gudgeon pin — a new chromed liner — a duraluminium piston fitted with a Dykes type piston ring (L shaped). At the time of writing this is known as the MCI kit and costs £23.00 (approx.). For the tuned version with parts already modified, known as the 9 part conversion, this costs £28.00 (approx.).

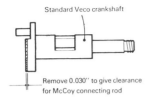

Standard Veco crankshaft

Remove 0.030″ to give clearance
for McCoy connecting rod

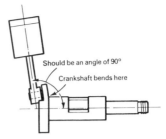

Should be an angle of 90°

Crankshaft bends here

Above: Fig 1 Providing clearance for McCoy connecting rod.

Left: Fig 2 Danger of bending crankshaft by starter.

These kits will give longer life and all that is needed normally is a new ring as stated earlier, the guide is that when the machining marks have disappeared from the surface which travels in the bore of the liner the ring should be replaced, as against £6.00 (approx) for the standard Veco Piston and liner assembly. The standard crank needs modifying to fit these kits as in Fig 1 to clear the connecting rod and help return the balance of the engine due to the lighter piston. It may be best to fit the Stroker Crank (cost £14.00 approx) but see later. Bearings do not normally give trouble, due to the engine RPM of 25,000 to 26,000, it is wise to gear the car for these sort of revs.

2. **Mechanical efficiency:** (Reducing friction). In the previous chapter you will find that the American Veco has a relieved piston as standard. The McCoy kit has running clearance also, so nothing needs to be done in this direction. The connecting rod needs checking using the jigs described in the previous chapter.

One fault I have found from time to time is that if an engine is flooded, when using a powerful starter, there is a danger of bending the crankshaft, just by the crankpin (see Fig 2). The method I use to check for this fault is to fit the connecting rod and view from the side to check for an angle of 90 degrees between crankshaft and piston (Fig 2). I suppose a checking jig could be made for this operation, but I find the sight method works quite adequately. If the crankshaft is bent a great deal of friction will develop.

The McCoy stroker crank is a good deal stronger in this respect, and if pennies permit, would be a good investment. This also brings the engine to almost 3.5 cc. End float should also be checked and corrected if any error (as in the previous chapter).

3. **Volumetric Efficiency:** (Getting more fuel mixture in): The induction period length can be increased, by removing from the crankshaft window, by the amounts in Fig 3. The carburettor bore, which is a compromise between good acceleration and top speed, should have a cross sectional area of 38 sq mm or a bore of 7 mm, this is without any intrusions in the throat such as spray loss, etc, and the bore will have to be increased to make allowance for these. The carb that seems about right is the Perry 40, to fit this

Fig 3 Removing metal from the crankshaft window.

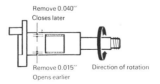

Remove 0.040″
Closes later

Remove 0.015″   Direction of rotation
Opens earlier

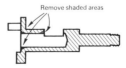

Remove shaded areas

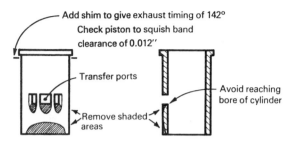

Fig 4 Modification of transfer ports and adding a shim.

you will have to increase the bore in the crankcase slightly or if finances allow, I find the PB carb works very well. This has a bore of 9/32 in just slightly over 7 mm. Consideration must be given to an efficient air filter even though it cuts down the air flow. Silicone sealant is the best material to glue the carb into the crank case.

The transfer ports on the standard liner should be modified as in Fig 4 as also could be the transfer ports on the McCoy MCI but keep away from the chrome on the bore of the liner. A shim may be fitted between the cylinder flange and the crankcase (Fig 4) to give an exhaust period of 142 deg, check with a degree disc.

An exhaust system, at silencer, should be one of the larger types available for cars to ensure minimum restriction to exhaust gases.

Combustion and Thermal Efficiency: As both these are directly related I will discuss them under one heading.

A high compression head gives a slight increase in performance but the main advantage is in giving a reliable tickover. These are available ready made, have a wider squish band, which increases turbulence to be fitted with your own heat sink or are available as a heat sink head from PB Products.

The plug type which I found best for the Veco is the Fox $1\frac{1}{2}$ volt idle bar but no doubt others will be just as effective, everyone I speak to regarding plugs do have their own views. All I can say is find a plug that suits you and stick with it.

Fuel mixes also cause a great deal of discussion again, I use 20% caster oil — 10% nitro-methane — 70% methanol.

For the beginner and also the more experienced the Veco 19 with McCoy conversion is probably the best value for money in the long term and will give quite a few hours of reliable practice and competition, which is required by us all to become and also stay competitive with the best drivers in the hobby.

At a later date I hope to give performance graphs and details of tests carried out on standard and converted Veco 19 as I have just completed an Engine Testing Dynamometer capable of absorbing $1\frac{1}{2}$ Brake Horse Power and revolving at 50,000 RPM 'Bearings Permitting'. It should be interesting to put all the engines through their paces and obtain test figures for all of them at varying loads and speeds.

6: Radio Stock Car Association

A FAST expanding r/c car section is that governed by the Radio Stock Car Association which has formulated rules, very much on the lines of full size Stock Car Racing as to design and construction, and with special attention to a limited cost formula. This limit, plus the robut nature of the stock car formula, plus the simpler nature of track requirements, means that a much larger pool of potential enthusiasts exists. The teenager still enjoying the novelty of his first wage packets and the young married man following his hobby on a budget can meet on level pocket terms with only individual skills between them.

Another stock car benefit is that the increased ground clearance enables a driver to practice on any reasonably level site, including the lawn at home, assuming he is also complying with silencer regulations of not more than 80dB at 30 ft — or rather less than the average small garden motor mower.

The track requirements are essentially simple. There should be an outer oval of 'fencing' boards about 6 in high to contain the cars which bounce off them on contact. Inner fence need only be of 2 in x 1 in strip laid flat on the ground. Sections can be a few feet long only, joined together with hooks and eyes or other type of snap fastener; outer fence of course will have small supporting feet, either attached or easily removable. The whole set-up for a track should go in the back of a fair sized estate car or small van. How elaborate it is is up to the club; inner fence can be painted up brightly, outer fence either plain or white or could be enlivened weith decals. Size depends very much on space available. If we consider a full size lap length going round, for example a football

Below: Stock car meeting in Holland. Their rules have now been amended to ban use of outside rollover bars (only to protect the paintwork!).

Left: The only gold top! Dave Wragg's car the only one with a gold top, as entitled, being the National Champion's machine. In other resects quite standard: it is the driver all along with stox.

pitch, we arrive at about 400 yards per lap. Model cars are ⅛th scale, so track can scale down to a mere 50 yards circuit as a minimum, with an oval up to twice this length as ideal.

Too big a circuit tends to spoil the fun with not enough cars in close proximity most of the time. If we consider six car events then a 50 yard lap allows an eight yard interval if all spaced out evenly, which is not what participants and spectators really want to see.

Interest has spread quickly to a number of countries in Europe, with Holland leading the way in numbers and enthusiasm, Sweden coming into the picture too, with promises of spiked tyres and ice events in the long winter months (we have yet to see this!).

Below: The track, showing the outer boards and lower inner track outline, with cars taking part in a heat. Some of the interested crowd can be seen behind the rope barrier.

The Cars . . .

At the moment two manufacturers head the market, notably Mardave, who were first in the field, and to whom most of the initial work in forming the association and devising the models must be credited; then there is Ke'jon who make a very similar car (naturally enough within a quite close formula!) and finally there is the Puma, which again follows the nearly standard pattern.

Cars are offered with a square section steel frame chassis already spot welded, to which components must be added, including nerf bars (to fend off the opposition!) rear springing — a sprung axle at the rear and a belt drive from the engine is a special stockcar feature — and the usual steering gear, wheels and so on. Normal clutch common to all r/c cars is used but brakes are not fitted. A one-piece moulded body is included, which will have to be finished, windows cut out, painted, and decorated.

Beginners might get the idea from looking at the kits that it is all too easy and that they can get some square section steel in the same size and weld it up in no time. But take care! Unless you already have some experience of this work it is quite a problem and most of the 'homemade' chassis we have seen looked terrible and performed that way.

In the next chapter we take readers through the building of a typical stock car and getting it running. Here, we offer details of the Radio Stock Car Association's Construction Rules and Procedure. For those who seek more knowledge direct then drop a line to John Orton, 49 Prince Albert Drive, Glenfield, Leicester who is the secretary; or to Chairman Dave Wragg, 1 Bignal Drive, Leicester Forest East, Leicester. Main racing centre at the moment is Newbridge, Nr. Leicester.

Making a Stock Car Circuit   An Outer Track Surround

This is a must, if you don't want a claim made against your club for injuries caused by cars taking off from the track into spectators.

The first steps in providing an outer track barrier is to go to your local tyre dealers and obtain some worn out tyres, a lot of these will be needed unless you are lucky enough to have a pair of bolt croppers, then you are able to cut the tyres in half.

With this method you are left with a big problem, a large pile of old tyres, which, without storage space on site, means someone having to move them every meeting to a storage area where they will not be a nuisance as a pile of old tyres is not a very wonderful sight.

This now brings me onto a better track surround. Although a little cost is involved it is a far better and safer method of keeping cars inside the track area.

Below: Methods of joining track boards. These are in short lengths for easy transport and stowage.

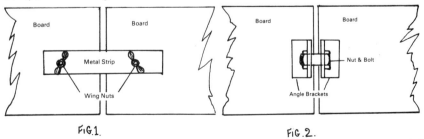

Fig.1.   Fig.2.

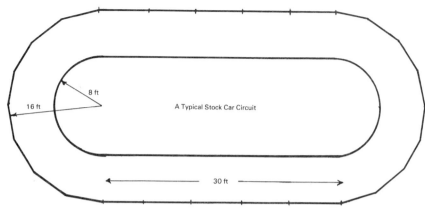

Above: Typical track dimensions and shape of track, which needs little more room than, say, a tennis court.

All that is required is plenty of 4 inch minimum high timber, the thickness is up to the individual, I recommend 1 inch thick timber as this will last a lot longer although I have seen $\frac{1}{8}$ inch toughened hardboard used but the replacement rate of boards was very high.

The total length of timber required will be 156 feet, as this is the total circumference of the outer perimeter give or take a few inches.

Constructing the boards to lengths of 6 feet, one should find that these are a nice size for storage and transporting.

Joining them together is not very hard, there are many ways in which this can be done for a few ideas see Figs 1 and 2.

Below: Rugged strength of stock cars can be judged from this row of five cars lined up before a recent meeting.

Marking the Inner Edge of the Track

This also can be done in many ways, some ways resulting in damage to the cars steering servo, even with a servo saver fitted.

The best way to mark the track, if you can get permission from the site owners, is to paint a line with road marking paint, this will not damage steering servos but I must admit that it will not be a very good deterrent to those drivers who like to cut corners.

Another way of marking the inner perimeter is with the use of the old tyres, this method will stop corner cutting and will not have any bad effect on the cars, only the bend need be marked with this method as should a driver wish to use the centre of the track at any time, then they would not have to worry about avoiding old tyres in the middle of the straight.

Yet another method is with the use of timber, this time the timber is laid flat on the track, although this method will require some time to be spent on it· with regards to bending the timber to an oval shape and making up a few connecting pieces.

These were only a few ideas as to how to mark out the track, they all have things for and against them, it is really up to the club's own choice . . .

Where the Tracks are:

MENCAP lies at the entrance to Western Park on the Hinckley Road (south) into Leicester. This is the RSCA track and does not have a club attached.

BATCHELOR BOWLES is another Leicester circuit, situated on the premises of the engineering firm of that name in Freeman Common Road, Leicester, near the Cattle Market.

NEWBRIDGE is the first purpose built circuit in the U.K., built by Wes Raynor of Mardave, and lies in a former railway cutting at the junction of B5380 road from Desford to Kirby Muxloe with the road going up to Ratby and Groby. These are all villages to the east of Leicester.

KEIGHLEY has a track at Marley in the grounds of the Keighley & District M.E.S., of which the Stock Car Section is a part.

CHESSINGTON have the use of a car park circuit on most Sundays at the RAF Rehabilitation Centre at Chessington.

HAYWARDS HEATH have Sunday use of a car park.

Since layout of a Stock Car Circuit is simple many new clubs may well be springing up on week-end car park sites which have not been reported to us. News of such is covered regularly in *Radio Control Model Cars*.

7: Assembling and Running a Stock Car

These building notes are offered as supplementary to 'official' instructions and as useful source material to those still in a state of 'armchair' modelling prior to making a practical start.

THREE CHOICES are normally available to the prospective r/c stock car racer in the shape of kits from Mardave Ke'Jon and Puma. Mardave was first in the field and offers the lowest priced kit; for several pounds more Ke'Jon provide a slightly more finished chassis frame — nerf bars being already fitted — and a working drawing in lieu of building instructions. This may be less comprehensible to the beginner than words and pictures! Finally for the racer eager to get into the driving seat right away Puma offer their kit ready assembled with only the radio to install plus engine etc, for very little above kit price. This is the answer to those who just want to race and never mind how the gear goes together. The final solution will probably be to run what the local club you are joining favours. In any event if you have the club already to join you will find opportunities of buying a used car from a member, or even find a fanatic builder who will put it together for you.

This is NOT the recommended thing! The mere assembling of the car in itself helps the beginner to understand what it is all about. Besides which making things is fun! Unless a hobby provides just that there seems no other reason to take it up. In our case we are making up a Mardave, with occasional interjections where Ke'Jon may differ in detail.

Mardave chassis comes unpainted and can be inspected for excellence or otherwise of spot welded joints. First task is to give it a good clean with Gunk or similar de-greasing fluids since it will normally have an oily film to prevent rust whilst in stock. Then go over it carefully with a fine file and emery paper to smooth the toughness of welds. Do not be too vigorous in removing metal, particularly round the engine mounting plates, but be sure not to leave any sharp edges or roughage that can cause cuts and scratches later.

Two lengths of strip metal are included to make up nerf bars on each side. These are secured with nuts and bolts, including two long bolts which must be bent slightly to act as stand off supports on each side. File sharp bits off these parts, too, before bolting them on. Front and rear nerf bars are in the form of steel rods, threaded at each end. These must be bent to shape. Those for the rear in a convenient 'handle' shape to form a shallow 'U'. Front bar is higher one side than the other, coming down in a sharpish slope, again threaded.

Front and rear bumper bars which form parts of the chassis are not drilled to take these overriders so that it is simpler to bend them first and drill to take them than to drill and have to bend to fit! Even so they will require a bit of manoeuvring to get into the holes. Nuts are included and one should be run up each threaded portion as far as it will go to locate the bars on the bumpers, leaving enough protruding through the bottom to take the retaining nut in each case. Suggestion is made in the building instructions that they may be screwed in place or soldered. Soldering alone may make a messy joint, if you decide to do it this way, use Baker's Fluid rather than a paste flux as it helps the run better with steel. Wash off vigorously after use.

Since these bars are not intended to be removed for any reason during the life of the car a little Loctite on each screw before running up the nut is a good thing. Then file off flush with top of nut and there is another neat non-scratch job.

Steering wishbones, kingpins and steering pivot arms follow very much the same pattern as for racing car assemblies already described and can be duly mounted on chassis. Ke'Jon assembly varies slightly from Mardave and drawing should be studied very carefully as wishbones come under chassis. Remember to use file and emery paper on parts before assembly to smooth out any roughness.

At this stage the chassis can be placed on a sheet of newspaper, propped up on wood blocks and given an undercoat of paint. Ideally, red oxide or similar base paint for metal should be used. I tend to use up odd quantities of any old aerosol paint that I have by me and use intended paint for second and third coats. Do not get paint on stub axles. These will probably have a touch of rust on them and should be polished up with old emery paper, a little Rustovent if available, and a touch of oil with retaining nuts screwed on temporarily with their washers, to be sure everything is to hand.

Now comes the part where stock cars differ materially from out-and-out formula and GT kits. Driving wheels at the rear are fully sprung. Mardave have two plastic mouldings together with what look like outsize clothes peg springs. The rear axle goes through one hole and the other hole serves for a bolt to secure to the chassis. On the inside of the chassis frame the large toothed driving wheel is located. Do not be in a hurry to complete this assembly if it is new to you. Take time to examine it thoroughly, like a wire puzzle, and get the hang of how it is going to work.

At the same time the engine to be used should be tried for size on the mounting plates which must be fitted to the engine retaining block. You will probably be using a Veco 19 so that fitting and drilling of engine bolting down holes presents no special problems. Bolt engine in place loosely. Put toothed belt over the big driving gear so that its ultimate location on gear which forms part of the clutch bellhousing can be assessed. Remove engine now and install flywheel clutch and clutch bellhousing. You will already

Below: A fine degree of individual treatment is evident in this line up of the Stockcar Racing Club of Holland.

Above: Rear springing, belt drive, bellcrank location and side nerf bars are clearly shown in this posed picture.

Left: Newcomer to the engine range. Competitively priced Fuji with schneurle porting and silencer (whether to the quietness limit is doubtful!):

have noted that there is not likely to be a great deal of clearance, in fact the chassis frame member on that side plays quite a part in keeping the belt in place. Fitting these parts has been dealt with already for racing cars and there is no difference here. In view of the very limited clearance available be sure that parts are well bedded down and screwed up good and tight. I wondered at first if it was going to fit in, but alarm unnecessary, it does!

Fitting of wheels and tyres is next operation — though most people will have put them roughly together just to see how it is going to look. As you will know both wheels and tyres have to be coated with an impact adhesive of which either Evostik or its Dunlop equivalent can be used. I like the latter since it is slightly slower in setting, but this is a personal preference, and the latest Evostik packing does claim increased adjusting time.

Do the wheels one at a time, spread adhesive on one hub then on inside of one tyre and slide it on. It is a messy job at the best of times, but can be eased a bit if you retain one of the plastic envelopes in which parts for the car come and use it as a glove for the hand slipping on the tyre. It helps too, if you rig up a threaded bolt of similar diameter in a drill which you can hold in a vice — ordinary hand-drill — then you can turn it round as you're fitting the tyre and get it nicely and evenly on. There is bound to be some surplus adhesive on you and on the tyre. This can most easily be removed with a rag dipped in petrol. There are so called solvents on the market but nothing really beats petrol. This is a tip from Wes Raynor of Mardave who has probably put on as many tyres as anybody. With some skins petrol tends to dry and crack them, so if you're one of them, rub some lanolin cream in afterwards.

Whilst the hand-drill is in use it is a good scheme to touch the edges of each tyre on a sheet of glass paper to take off the sharp corner, rounding them very slightly. Later you may wish to have several sets of wheels and tyres to suit track and weather conditions in varying degrees of hardness. But at the start this is not really needed, though a couple of spares would be a sensible item for the tool/spares box.

It will be noted that rear wheels bolt up with the main part of the axle of larger diameter, and are fixed with a nut. This gives a certain amount of play since there is no flat on which an allen screw can bed down, only the pressure of the nut against the wheel which in turn presses against the shoulder on the axle.

Front wheels should be fitted with minimum play. A tip is to insert a paper washer between wheel and holding nut, and then pull it off when secure, thus leaving just enough free movement. Be sure to adjust toe-in with at least 5 degrees on each wheel. A rough and ready angle adjustment is to draw a line at right angles to the axle line $3\frac{1}{2}$ inches long; at the $3\frac{1}{2}$ inch point measure in by $\frac{1}{16}$ in at a time, which amount is approximately one degree per $\frac{1}{16}$ in. There is a little error but no more than you will get in any measurement of this sort. All the things we say about wheels in another article are equally applicable to stock cars.

The track rod joining the front wheels will be the adjuster for toe-in. Mardave recommend that a V-shaped kink be bent into it to allow minor adjustment when it is in place and also to absorb any violent side swipes. One end of track rod can be bent up at right angles slipped into one of the holes ready drilled in the pivot arms — the two outside holes (ie, nearest the rear) should be used to take this track rod. I like to solder a washer on this bent up end leaving the other end with a threaded Kwik-link on it for fine adjustment. Most users will, I expect, prefer to leave the rod straight and have a Kwik link on each end as they require no soldering and fit in a jiffy. Those in the kit are plastic, others on the market are partly of metal, it is all a matter of favourite bits and pieces . . . no one sort can be offered as the best.

Steering bellcrank/servo saver can be connected up now to the steering assembly. Shortest simplest possible bending up is recommended. Location in the holes provided on the bellcrank will adjust the amount of turn given to the steering. Do not necessarily take the most possible, it makes the car trickier to drive and only enough to go round is really needed. If you are building Mardave your servo will be right up by the steering and offer no problems. Throttle servo will be located in the hollow of the L-shaped radio box provided, and again connection to the engine bellcrank is of the simplest and shortest.

Plastic tank can next be fitted. A very simple rubber harness holds it in place. It should be possible to get some wide rubber bands from a good stationer who will normally order a box ($\frac{1}{4}$ lb weight seems smallest) which should very nearly provide enough for a club! Connection from tank to engine is via neoprene tube. Check that size provided is what you want — there are at least two different sizes. It should be cut in middle and a fuel filter inserted. Type should be easily unscrewed and taken apart for regular cleaning out of muck. Just as undesirable if not more so is track dirt, burnt

Below left: Front steering wishbones on Ke'Jon stock car are located one above and one under chassis frame. Below right: Mardave wishbones are both under frame with track rod above. Both makes have sprung front wheels.

rubber and the like getting into the engine through the carburettor opening so that a filter is needed here. A wide variety of types are available from simple plastic foam, which acts better with a little oil soaking, to quite elaborate honeycomb devices. Or there is the simpler method of a piece of silk stretched over the opening and held down with a light piano wire ring as a circlip. But do filter, otherwise life of engine may be much shorter than you had hoped.

If engine is new, now is a good time to give it a tankful of fuel, running it as rich as you can at tickover speed. Ten to fifteen minutes, or a good tankful should take care of running in. Chassis can be cleaned down, radio box fitted in place and radio and battery installed. Too much reliance should not be placed on 'servo tape' which holds down parts being sticky on both surfaces. It is better to wrap receiver and battery in foam sheet, rubber band them, and wedge in radio box with further foam offcuts. Servos can best be fixed with the attachments usually provided. They are quite robust physically and well protected from knocks by the stout chassis and sheet support on which radio box rests. Aerial is taped to underside of radio box, or holes can be drilled in box lid to provide an even lacing of the aerial wire. This should be adequate for reception, but there is nothing to stop you fitting up a flexible tube or 'snake' to stick up out of the car carrying the aerial wire. Whatever you do, maintain the length as supplied. Should you use a stiff wire aerial (with an eye protecting loop at the end, please!) make sure length of this wire plus what is left of original aerial equals length first provided. Be sure to insulate **bare** wire from chassis.

You will no doubt have already fitted your heat sink. This may well be the very neat and simple type provided by Mardave. You will probably wish to trim it slightly so that body fits over comfortably. Smaller thicker types should go in unmodified. Body is a good stout moulding and requires only window openings to be cut and fixing clips to be added before painting. Cut outs can be done with a handrill to start a hole and then go round the opening with a fretsaw, or can be removed with a hot soldering iron. Try this method out first on a bit of scrap plastic to see how fast your iron softens and goes through the material, and generally get a little practice in. Windscreen, rear and side window shapes are a matter of personal choice. However, if you provide good window

Below: Spring-loaded self-centring on Steve Busby stocker. Deep U steering override link can just be seen.

Above: Elegant paint job on a Danish stock car. More for show than use perhaps, as the hood is not painted in standard style.

shapes at the side a great deal of adjustment can be done without removing body, and tank can be filled via rear window. This can be achieved without any loss of realism or weakening of the body.

Rules require that beginners paint hoods white down to the waistline, changing colours progressively as you go up the skill scale. Only other rule requirement is that your name should appear on side. There is however no reason why body should not be made interesting. It will have a hard life so that full customising except for a special 'show piece' body is not recommended. Any number of colourful decals can be obtained — SG do a very good sheet — and bright finishes, zig-zag patterns and so on have the very useful purpose of making your car stand out well during a race and avoid that grim business of finding you have been apparently driving someone else's car! You might even find some local tradesman who would sponsor you in a minor way for carrying his name on your car . . .

Outside Roll bars are not allowed in the RSCA rules though permitted in Holland.

There is no structural reason for this, just that the careful Dutch do not want to risk scratching some of their elegant paint jobs!

Final comments: Do not be tempted to use really hot fuel for stock car racing. It wears out engines more quickly without worthwile results and costs more. Use a good old 'cooking' variety of about 10% nitro. Many newcomers will already have had experience of glow plug running from model aircraft use and need only remember that running on the dirty ground introduces special problems that the clean upper air does not. Clean down car and chassis after racing as thoroughly as you can. Do not leave fuel in tank or engine. Trickle charge starter battery every few weeks even if you have not been using it much; the same goes for radio batteries and glow plug accumulator.

What you need for Stock Car Racing

1. A Club to Join (or start).
2. A Track to use — make friends with local schools, car park people (big factories, stores) — a few DIY members can make up the oval circuit boards.

3. A stock car kit — your local dealer will let you see Mardave kit (which complies with RSCA construction rules) or Ke'Jon (which requires slight modification to comply).

4. Two-channell radio Tx and Rx (Futaba, Sanwa, MacGregor, you name it).

5. Engine (Veco, Fuji or perhaps the Irvine).

6. Engine starter (Sullivan, Kavan or make your own).

7. Accumulator 12 volt (Varley, or ex-car, motorcycle, or any to come).

8. Smaller $1\frac{1}{2}$/2v accumulator for glow plugs (or tap off accumulator).

9. Fuel (not too hot — good 'cooking' quality).

10. Operating licence (£2.80 for **five** years).

11. Loads of enthusiasm and a sense of humour!

Below: Internal view, this time on a scratch built car built by Alan Hobbs of Redhill, who made it during an evening class session.

8: Steering Geometry

Oversteer and Understeer

A CAR oversteers when it responds more freely than intended to a turn of the front wheels. What happens then is that the driving wheels at the rear instead of pushing the car forward in a straight line, as when the front wheels are not turned, continues to push forward as before, but the front wheels are no longer directly in front but to one side. This encourages the rear end to spin out and the already turned front wheels give added encouragement. The inside wheels tend to lift and may well roll the car; at the best the spin out slows, stops, or otherwise impedes the forward progress of the car.

With understeer the car wants to continue on its straight line, and resists the turning movement of the front wheels. The driving force behind is stronger than the turning force in front. The **outside** wheels would try to lift in this case, but the inside wheels also want to lift in the circumstances. If these two forces can be balanced, an ideal situation exists for the creation of a four-wheel drift round the corner. In full-size racing practice this is the common practice, with model car racing it is only just beginning to be achieved by more skilful drivers — and even more important — more skilful setting up of the car beforehand.

What are the Influences?

What desirable changes can be made towards achieving the ideal condition? A number of factors are involved all of them contributing something to the solution. They are (not necessarily in order of importance).
1. Ackerman steering effect.
2. Toe-in of front wheels.
3. Caster of front wheels.
4. Camber of front wheels.
5. Tyres.
(a) Width.
(b) Hardness in relation to rear wheel tyres.
6. Chassis set-up and flexibility.

Ackerman Steering

It is obvious that in a turn the inside wheel of a pair travels a shorter distance. With a line of soldiers or dancers the inside soldier/dancer marks time whilst the outside person is very nearly running. Where steering arms are at right angles to the stub axles the slower moving inside wheel slips and is worn out more quickly whilst preventing a smooth turning action. If however they are angled inwards, so that if extended they would meet centrally at a point just in front of the rear axle, then by adjusting the location of the track rod along the converging lines of the steering arms a variable ratio

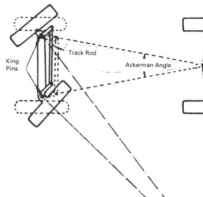

Above left: Ingenious method of achieving Ackermann steering with smaller circle described by inner wheels as used by PB International and US Delta amongst others. Above right: Ackermann Steering: Showing principle of smaller circle turned by inner wheel, harking back to coaching days when invented by German coachbuilder.

of radii can be arranged for each wheel. This is the simple approach to Ackerman steering. In practice to obtain any great difference in the respective radii track rod might have to be considerably shortened and become less effective and get in the way of other components.

This limitation has been overcome, for example, in the PB system where additional links are added, achieving the same purpose but keeping the track rod line close up to the front. The earlier PB cars in the Expert Series also tackled the problem with a sweep type steering link. If the angle of the steering arm is increased this brings the meeting point of the two converging arms if extended nearer the front of the car and means that a little cross movement of track rod produces a large amount of turn. This, however, does not give the practical solution of the two wheels turning about a common point but with different though related radii. All it does is offer two unrelated radii with some of the original problems of scrub unsolved.

Below left: Kingpin axis behind stub axle to provide a non-adjustable degree of positive caster. Below right: Kingpin axis on line of stub axle — more adjustable but harder to make.

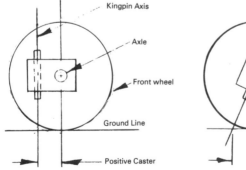
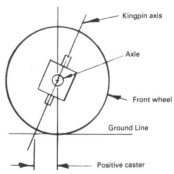

Indeed, it is possible to produce a position where additional toe-in is introduced to cancel too much difference in related turns!

Toe-in

This leads naturally to toe-in, or setting the front wheels slightly pigeon-toed. Do not be afraid of too much toe-in. It is quite difficult to see in a model as little as $2\frac{1}{2}$ degrees of toe-in. Be bold and give up to $5/7\frac{1}{2}$ degrees which seems an awful lot but will improve handling and smooth response. A very easy way to make the necessary adjustment is to draw a line equal to axle length wheel to wheel. Add two lines at right angles as far apart as the insides of your two wheels. Then $3\frac{1}{2}$ inches up these two new lines measure inwards in steps of $\frac{1}{16}$th in on each side. Join up the marks from the axle line base and you have a series of 1 degree steps or thereabouts. (The maths? Circumference of a circle is 2 Pi R or 2 x 22/7 x 7/2 x 16 which gives the answer in $\frac{1}{16}$ths of an inch as 352. There are 360 degrees in a circle and the difference could well be no more than the thickness of a pencil mark, or as accurately as one can reasonably draw it. No good for big angles of course but fair enough for little ones!)

In any corner the tendency is always for the inside wheel to try to lift off in an endeavour to mantain a straight line. For this reason racing 'chair' motor cyclists have their passenger lean over to the lifting wheel to counteract this with weight transference. Or, to take another example, banking a curve on a race track to enable cars to go round faster, that is, without the inside (or lower on the bank) wheel lifting.

Caster

Apart from toe-in there are other ways in which the wheels can be positioned in relation to the kingpins. These kingpins can be dead upright, like an old lady riding a bicycle, can be leaning backwards, or leaning forwards. A great many car kits for the sake of simplicity have the stub axle positioned behind the kingpins. This provides positive caster which is what we want. It helps to keep the wheels down by its forward rolling action, thus reducing in a small measure the lifting tendencies noted already in a turn.

This type of caster cannot be altered without making up a fresh pair of steering units. A more adjustable form has the line of the kingpins on the same axis as the stub axles, which has the disadvantage from the builder's point of view that it is rather more complicated to make. It is worth the trouble however as the degree of forward tilt can be adjusted to suit a particular car set up.

With kingpins and stub axles on the same line and upright, there would of course be no caster action at all, which would be a pity but certainly not a fatal defect!

Camber

Here is yet another way the wheel can be positioned. The top can lean inwards, which is negative camber; or outwards which is positive camber. The former is the more desirable since it tends to press more of the tyre surface on to the ground, hence greater adhesion. This will be acheved in two ways. If the stub axle is bent slightly this will have the desired effect, and tyres will wear to conform to their angle on the ground surface. Better perhaps is to leave the stub axle unchanged and adjust the angle of the kingpins to be very slightly inclined inwards.

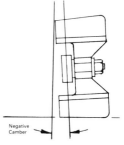

Negative Camber

These latter two alterations, caster and camber, will not solve problems of steering ina a miraculous way. In fact most drivers and manufacturers tend to ignore them, or give only slight importance to them. The painstaking constructor will take note of them.

Tyres

Current rules give wide latitude in the matter of tyre tread width — with 1 in minimum up to $2\frac{1}{2}$ in maximum. Less generous is diameter, minimum front being $2\frac{1}{4}$ in, rear $2\frac{1}{2}$ in. However, this should enable some considerable variations to be achieved before even considering the other important matter of tyre hardness. Usual practice is to have quite narrow tread at the front and massive width at the back. Normal range of tyre widths seem to run between $1\frac{1}{4}$ in width of tread (not making use of minimum 1 in tread!) to $2\frac{1}{2}$ in — the maximum. Diameters which are not controlled under BRCA rules at the top end, generally range between $2\frac{3}{4}$ in to $3\frac{1}{4}$ in. A good mix would be $2\frac{3}{4}$ in front tyres of $1\frac{1}{4}$ in width and $3\frac{1}{4}$ in dia rear $2\frac{1}{2}$ in tread.

This takes no account of tyre consistency which ranges from soft through to hard, and the actual make-up of the tyre compound. Soft tyres give more bite and have more actual tyre area on the ground to provide tractive effort, so will be found as the rear driving wheels equipment. Since understeer is better than oversteer front tyres will be harder, that is, have less bite, so that oversteer and spin out problems are avoided.

Two other factors will influence tyres to be used, namely track surface and weather conditions. Tracks vary very much in their surface, which itself will change during a weekend's racing by the deposit of rubber on its surface providing more adhesion and involving a change of tyres during a meeting, perhaps within an hour or two. Wet weather again involves tyre changes so that in some countries racing is stopped for the wet — notably in parts of USA where rain is less common than in the UK! British and cotinental drivers have tackled the problem successfully and racing goes on whatever the weather, though times are slower and cars lose adhesion. Softer rubber is the answer, but then tracks dry out during a race and all the 'fullsize' problems of 'do I fit rain tyres?' arise.

Tyres remain the least developed of model car accessories. They are stamped out from rubber of synthetic sheet, wasting some 60% of their content; have to be stuck to wheel hubs in a very 'un-mechanical' manner; wear out quickly; have no certainty of exact character from batch to batch. A number of substitute synthetics are being tried,

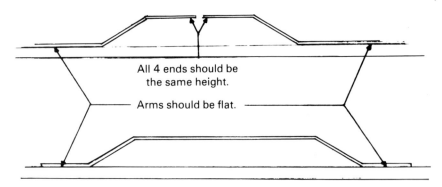

All 4 ends should be
the same height.

Arms should be flat.

there are a few moulded (but expensive) tyres in use, but so far no manufacturer has come up with a real answer, though there is a very good variety on offer both from domestic makers and from overseas. The experts swear by their own particular favourites, but there is no unanimity, nor have any of the fullsize manufacturers shown interest in producing a model racing tyre as yet.

Chassis Set-up and Flexibility

Last, but by no means least, of the problems of steering control is chassis set-up and flexibility. In the early days of r/c model car racing the chassis was designed solidly, with front and rear springing of a fairly complicated nature. As time went on the impossibility of a simple springing practice using a rigid chassis led to changes. Today, only in the case of stock car models is a rigid chassis fully sprung in use. For its purpose of fairly slow speed operation and ability to stand up to abuse it can hardly be bettered.

What has happened to high speed model racing cars is that two apparently irreconcilable objects have been built into the chassis. A rigid rear end is needed to transfer power evenly to the driving wheels, whilst a flexible front end to carry the steering is necessary so that the car will be able to iron out unevenness of ground and sometimes erratic steering commands without departing too much from its desired direction.

This was tackled in several ways. The American practice is very largely to have a really rigid rear power pod plate (up to $\frac{1}{16}$ in thick of aluminium) to which is bolted a lighter more flexible forward chassis plate. Some control of this flexibility is obtained via the radio (or shaker) plate which connects the two parts and provides both rigidity and flexibility to rear and front. British approach to high speed (via Keith Plested and

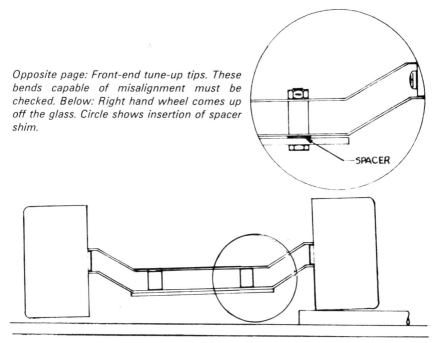

Opposite page: Front-end tune-up tips. These bends capable of misalignment must be checked. Below: Right hand wheel comes up off the glass. Circle shows insertion of spacer shim.

his group of experts for PB Products) was a sandwich chassis where a long V of metal was adhered to a normal chassis form. This provides a tapering off from rigid double thickness at the rear to less and less at the front — a kind of metal reinforcing gusset in fact. This has worked very well and continues to be enjoyed by what can be called the middle range of expert drivers.

It still did not provide the ideal solution. This was sought by Dutch designers who tried out a fibreglass/alloy sandwich but supply and production problems prevented full exploitation. Sweden had a try with an all plastic chassis but cost of moulding presented difficulties and only produced what was virtually a 'throw-away' chassis for short time use. Meanwhile Sabbatini of SG was working on a cut-and-try method of waisting a chassis hour glass fashion, good and broad at the back and slinky at the front.

This has been followed by most drivers who trim their chassis to what they think is the ideal shape. It works well but only when fitted to a given track or tracks. What suits one surface can be most disappointing elsewhere. PB Products now provide the compromise solution by offering their international kit with **two** separate chassis — one broad and one narrow, which latter can be further trimmed down to taste. A spot check on users at Lyons who had their own special widths resulted in an average difference of $\frac{1}{8}$th of an inch, standardising at approximately three inches wide at the narrowest part. That's consensus opinion!

Whatever approach you are making to the subject it is essential that, at rest, the chassis sits squarely on its four wheels, or you will have the 'wobbly table effect' of erratic running, taking a better turn on one hand than the other, and generally unsatisfactory running. A good checking surface is a sheet of plate glass. (For years I have had such a sheet with polished edges nicely rounded and used it as a surface plate — fairly cheap, easily replaced and nearly as good as the expensive metal type). If you lack this then try using a mirror laid flat on the table.

Gene Husting of Associated is very keen on this business of chassis 'tweaking' and devotes part of his instruction for RC100 to it, with suitable diagrams. I cannot do better than reproduce them with extracts and due acknowledgements to the author.

'Take a piece of $\frac{3}{8}$ in tubing and roll it under right hand front wheel. Note how far the left hand wheel comes off the glass. Do the same for the other wheel. Generally, one wheel will come higher off the glass than the other. This means chassis 'tweaked' to one side or the other. By holding the front and rear wheels, you should be able to twist or 'tweak' the chassis back to square. After running the car for a few minutes it may settle back to its 'tweaked' state. If this happens it will cause the car to have too much oversteer in one direction and too much understeer in the other. If this is so, instead of bending chassis back to shape put one or more washers between the chassis plate and lower cross arm, as shown. Place only as many washers as it needs to get the wheels to come off the ground the same amount left and right with the tubing test.'

Needless to say, the two rear tyres should be of same diameter as each other, and the front tyres ditto. The normal equal bends and flat surfaces of the front wishbones should also be above suspicion. As machine cut and jig bent items they may not always be absolutely true and should be carefully checked as the first suspected culprits of irregular running.

9: Axle Blocks and Stub Axles

IN WRITING of steering geometry quite a lot was said about the desirable arrangement of stub axles and steering blocks and this chapter goes a little further on the practical side by showing what some of the kit manufacturers have done to achieve their ends. These ends must be strictly divided between the wholly desirable and the limitations enforced by a production cost limitation.

The minimum need is for an axle on which the wheel can be placed and a suitable socket into which the axle can be placed. This socket must have a lever attached to it to enable the wheel to be steered. That's all! Regard must be given as to the location of these parts relative to one another. Is the axis of the kingpin to go through the axle line, or is the wheel to trail? If so how much? Can the amount of caster be readily altered? What is the ideal amount?

Obviously low and medium priced kits will have to solve the problem in the cheapest possible way. Perhaps producer prefers to economise here so that some detail such as ballbearing rear axle can be included and get inside the budget. Let us consider the simplest possible set up. This must undoubtedly be the GB kits put out by GB Models of Weston-super-Mare which incorporate a certain number of PB parts as well as their own specialities. Here, the axle is in the form of a bolt, sleeved for smooth running, which goes through a rectangular block. Kingpin goes through another hole drilled vertically in front of the axle line. The axle bolt also goes through the steering arm to hold it against the block. This steering arm is a flat strip of metal, twisted at right-angles (like a cheese straw) to bring its flat surface parallel with the ground for easy attachment of track rod. With its single bolt holding it can be displaced quite easily unless secured very tightly to the block and locked in place with Loctite or similar. Another small hole drilled and tapped in the block to enable an additional locking screw to be fixed might be advisable.

More common, and followed by several makers in even their de luxe kits, is a similar arrangement but using an L-section strip with alternative location holes drilled to take

Below left: 'Cheese straw' twist of the GB design – simplest of all methods. Below right: Straight through bolt with L-section steering arm is Associated answer.

Above left: A similar method used by Mardave, but with a plastic block and a sprung kingpin. Above right: Associated refinement using machined steering cross-beam. Note slot to take edge of L-section arm on the turn.
Advancement: PB's steering arm bolts firmly to axle block; kingpin runs in bearings, stub axle purpose made.

different track rod and steering arm locations. This is more robust, less liable to bending, though not so easily adjusted for Ackerman effect. It can be employed with simple strip type cross-beam or with the more elegant machined alloy or moulded nylon beams. Such beams, incidentally, are usually angled on the underside to provide a degree of caster angle. At least one firm is offering a choice of angles from 5-15 degrees. However, a change can simply be made by inserting wedges securely to produce required angle.

Mardave follow this block plus angle method with a couple of useful improvements. Their block is a plastic moulding and the kingpin is sprung to give a reasonable amount of movement to the front end, a useful addition to a low-priced kit where chassis is necessarily in one piece and more rigid than might otherwise be ideal.

Following the idea of a plastic moulding for the axle block, comes the next idea, namely, to mould the steering arm integrally with the block, and to incorporate a suitable sleeve through which kingpin can run. This is followed by all the 1/12th scale electric cars, possibly feeling that only moderate strength is required here anyway. The Italian SG goes a step further and provides wheels with double ballbearings. These are unshielded and may be troublesome to keep clean as well as costly when changing tyres

Below left: SG combine steering block and steering arm — a neat solution. Below right: Ultimate simplicity by Minicars — single casting for kingpin, steering arm and stub axle.

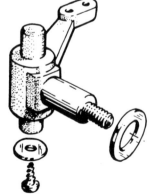

Above: Parts for the Delta unit. Here axle block and steering arm are machined from a single block (now a single casting). Wheel has double ball bearings. Right: The simple parts making up the PB original 'Experts' style unit.

if a whole stock of such wheels must be carried. If content with low priced bearings some surplus firms such as Whistons of New Mills Stockport should usually be able to oblige.

It is interesting to find that Keith Plested pioneered an 'engineering' solution in Britain (at the same time Bill Campbell of Delta was doing much the same thing in U.S.A.). Answer is a stout flat steering arm plate which bolts **under** the rectangular steering block. The block is reversible for left and right hand use; one additional tapped hole is made to enable it to lock in place with a screw, and kingpin holds it firm. This is the pattern that appeared on the first Expert series kits.

Final evolution, as seen on PB Internationals is the wholly machined steering block, where block and steering arm are formed from a single piece of metal. It involves a number of separate operations but the end product is well worth the effort. Here an added refinement appears. Instead of ball racing the wheels, PB have ballraced the stub axle with two **shielded** ballraces to keep out the dirt. Wheel is locked in place on the axle via a rollpin and axle goes round.

Below left: The Delta unit duly assembled. A single attachment only to cross-beam will be noted. Below right: PB International answer. Single machined unit for steering arm and axle block. Two piece kingpin enabling straight through stub axle, running in double ball bearings — wheel pinned.

The American Delta kit also employs a one piece block/steering arm, which would seem to predate the PB. It follows very closely the pattern of the PB Expert part but is made in one piece. It looks very much as though machining operations have been simplified. Perhaps it has been possible to make use of some already commercially available extrusion and work from there. Delta up to date (I have not seen their very latest offering) use a plain bolt axle in the usual way without attempting to fit races here. They go (as with SG) in the wheel hubs and are shielded. Other differences that will be noted are positions of kingpins. PB have split their kingpin in two with one piece coming down and the other going up to permit axle to go through line of kingpin. Delta is a simple trailing axle with single piece kingpin.

The ultimate simplicity award must go to Minicars' Challenger. Here a single casting provides kingpin, which rotates in the cross beam, steering arm and stub axle. Two separate moulds are required in manufacture for left and right hand and its production must be expensive bearing in mind the possible quite limited number required. I do not have any information on its strength in use since very few kits have been seen in England. The fact that Minicars' man Per Gustafsson was European champion for Sports GT in 1977 should be some guarantee of its practical value. (Though he did win on a mainly Associated car!)

10: The Kitmasters . . .

TO BE successful in the top ranks of model car racing the driver must rely on one of three great kit manufacturers, alphabetically, Associated from California, PB Products of England, and SG Racing of Italy. These three makes have dominated the contest scene throughout the world for several seasons now, with victory see-sawing from one to the other in a delightfully open way. Who are the people behind the scenes — or on stage for that matter? All three firms are run by designer-driver-maker proprietors, managing directors, or top men. Associated have Gene Husting a name usually found high up on Californian contest reports, who also writes valuable technical articles on engine tuning, chassis design for the U.S. model press (and happily now allows us to quote him!) PB Products who in 1977 have topped their Expert series with the amazing International have Keith Plested at the head of things, ably assisted by son Mark who likes the speed aspect (he runs a superbike!) but is less interested in the mechanics of how and why. Keith could so easily have been champion of Europe this summer but for .. always a but for . . . you must finish to win! His name too will most times be found amongst the finalists — three times second in the British Championships this season. Then we come to Italy's Franco Sabattini (the S of SG: Garafoli is the G. Father G produces the Super Tigre range of engines, son Leonardo works with Franco) who is the youngest of the three kit masters. He races like a true Italian with every ounce of energy

PB International as made up by comparative novice. Seen mid-summer at Catfoss still clean and unsullied.

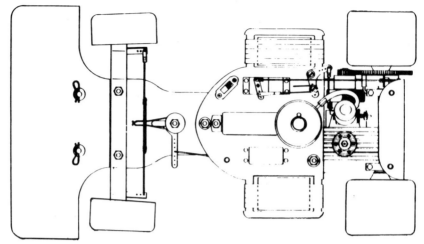

Above: Line drawing of RC100. This show layout, radio plate, Johnson Chicken Hopper tank, radio and servo locations. Steering servo has been installed inverted — a quite usual practice.

and zest desperate to win to the very last lap. He has been Champion of Europe, and his cars have also been the tools of other champions, Rony Ton and Colonna.

So much for the personal background. Gene and Keith have developed their cars gradually over the years, with the help of enthusiasts whose ideas have been worked in where practical, the subtle refinement that comes only with race proven cars that evolve rather than be instant brainwaves. Franco has been more of a lone wolf producing a splendid car to suit his own racing style, to which users must conform if they are to be successful.

The Chassis

No one of these three can be said to have followed another's lead. Their chassis are all distinctively different. To achieve the desired state of rigidity at the back and flexiblity at the front Associated have a power pod, almost square and $\frac{1}{8}$ in thick to house the motor and rear assembly, to which is attached a more flexible front end. Above this is the radio plate which plays a significant part in the transition from rigid to flexible by a designed amount of play in the front fixing. I must add here that the power pod is a beautifully prepared piece of work, superbly drilled and slotted, the result of a great deal of on circuit development, and well worth the polishing which the designer urges upon users!

Keith Plested approaches the chassis problem in quite a different way. His Expert chassis features a sandwich of two pieces of alloy, one rectangular the other tapering to a point like a gusset of metal. This provides stiff at the back, flexible at the front. Out of this arose the International chassis, which comes as two alternative pieces, one for smooth circuits, which is fairly broad and stiffish, the other a slimmer job altogether for rough circuits. Drivers then waist the front ends to suit their special requirements, coming to a thinnest measurement across of as little as three inches. This seems the concensus width over a number measured — all within an eighth of an inch.

Franco Sabattini is a devotee of the flexible chassis, thinning his own until it is almost too frail to hold together — or so his opponents hope. This ultra flexible approach brings its own special problems. What about the rear end? Here Franco has his own novelty in the shape of a second bearing to take the tip of the engine crankshaft so that it is supported at both ends, by the main holding down bolts of the crankcase and this extra bearing. On the under side of the chassis is a protective strip to save the gear should tyre wear endanger it (Keith could have used one in 1977 at Lyons!) His new Professional kit is less whippy and this extra support for the crankshaft has been dropped, though there is still a stout gear protector underneath.

Brakes

Disc brakes were first introduced to r/c model cars by the Swiss firm of Brem, but PB were quick to appreciate their virtues with power output increasing beyond control unless improved braking could permit flat out runs down ever lengthening straights. It has proved immensely successful. Latest SG now includes it on the Professional kit and it is offered as an alternative on the Associated RC100. Indeed, one German accessory firm has been listing it as a special for some time — presumably their own product — to fit the RC100.

Clutch

Thirty years ago I was racing cable cars (they were fast with up to 10cc motors, young man, and were tethered to a central pylon — speeds up to 150 mph ... really!) which used an identical clutch to that, in principal, used today, namely centrifugal in action with shoes that swung out to make contact with the bellhousing when a sufficient speed was attained. Development of the flywheel, clutch and bellhousing assembly is therefore relatively ancient but until recently somewhat stagnant.

Basic method of two shoes with a horseshoe shaped spring regulating the resistance to throwing out speed is used by both Associated and PB with minor variations. PB have the simpler assembly. Associated has now moved over from specially hardened alloy shoes to bent up metal shoes which make metal to metal contact, omitting the traditional brake lining inside the bellhousing. This is a controversial move that may not stand up to the high speeds now being obtained with a well 'breathed upon' K & B, though adequate for 'cooking' engines.

Below left: Stout metal protector fitted to SG Expert kit. Note also slot for disc of brake, now featured. Below right: SG disc brakes. Operation is quite different from that of the PB International.

Sabattini is now using either hard wood or tufnol type shoes, ie, not metal at all, held in place with a circlip, which goes right round the shoes, fitting into a shallow groove provided. This is a much simpler solution than the horseshoe springs which always looked untidy and unmechanical. Only a season's racing will prove the merits or otherwise. It should be possible to vary tension very easily with a series of different strength circlips, without the risk of losing vital bits on the pit floor.

Steering

Here we have a definite breakthrough for PB International which offers the most elegant and practical steering unit of all. The Expert series provided a neat system with a slot taking the turns, and adjustable toe-in available with an eccentric connection to the stub-axle assembly, but the International goes one further with full Ackermann benefits of differential radii for the inner wheel on a turn. SG have very neat stub-axle-kingpin units and have reintroduced an amount of springing to the front wheels. The very latest offering from Bologna is a centrally fixed unit that pivots centrally and should in theory be able to keep both wheels on the ground at most times.

Finally, the standard RC100 steering assembly which has been identical with all the RC range from RC2 on, is giving place to an alloy cross piece (like the nylon one on the PB Expert or the alloy Marker unit) where the track rod is actuated by prongs touching twin ballbearings to produce a very sweet unit. This I believe was first fitted at Pomona on the occasion of the World Championships when it was noticed how well the PB Internationals were faring...

Dave Martin comments:

'The steering system on RC100 is way behind PB in design (and Delta) but it really is the most robust and reliable system on any car on the market. I ran RC100 for one and a half years and never had any trouble with it — it is really typical Associated: about twice as big, and strong than it really needs to be (believe me reliability is the way to win). It is, however, rather limited in performance, the trailing axles slow down the steering response due to high servo load. Also the servo saver itself has a rather undesirable design fault since the sprung piano wire forks, even when set to maximum

Below left: This is the PB disc brake connected to servo for both braking and throttle with a stout rocker movement. Disc is substantially housed and well protected from shunts. Below right: SG clutch uses hard wood or tufnol for shoes which are held in place with a circlip. Changes in weight and material has taken place with some lightening.

Above: Associated clutch, shoes and bellhousings. On right are hard anodised aluminium; on left latest steel shoes. These have 3/32 in split-spring pins in place of earlier (and fiddling) 1/16 in pins. Bellhousing is unlined with metal-to-metal contact in this version.

safe tension, will still always break away from the bell crank by an amount proportional to the side load and this causes valuable steering lock to be lost.

This is due to the fact that the resistance to 'break away' increases proportional to the distance the spring fork is forced away from the bellcrank, (ie the amount of movement lost). This lost lock manifests itself in a nasty high speed understeer, because at high speed the side forces are the greatest. On the PB steering system the design of the servo-saver means that the servo is directly coupled to the wheels right up to the maximum servo load (about $4\frac{1}{2}$ lbs). Therefore there is no loss of lock at all unless the wheels happen to hit a bump etc, which is the reason we have servo savers in the first place. I've always considered this to be the main reason why the PB has better high speed handling — rather than its Ackerman geometry, which obviously helps but I'm sure its effect isn't the same magnitude as that due to the servo-saver (the in-line kingpin — stub axle set-up also helps the PB system over the RC100).'

Wheels and Tyres

Associated get full marks for offering their wheels and tyres already glued up and ready for use. It is a messy job gluing on tyres and can be done badly. As a factory product with balancing facilities all the wheel/tyre units are decently balanced and cleaned up. (They won't last for ever and it is only putting off the evil day of course). In general wheels and tyres are the same for all, with minor fixing variations. I prefer a nice accessible allen screw tightened down on a ground flat rather than fumbling through a tyre edge to find the holes. Again Associated score here.

SG seem to have been experimenting with their tyres. Some seem to be natural rubber: other would appear to have been cut off a tube, which is economical though not too highly regarded by the experts. One pair looks very much as if it had been rolled and

Left: PB steering. This is a real bull point! Not only does the ball joint and track rod kit provide true Ackermann steering, but machining of axle blocks provides a really workmanlike assembly.

stuck at an angled joint, another economy measure, but one which should not be unacceptable if joining is well done.

In any event drivers have their own particular fancies with tyres and build up a stock for all eventualities. What comes with the car will undoubtedly be used. Hubs all look very much alike and are moulded — no one in the kit field here is sending out spun alloy or other de-luxe styles!

Fuel Tanks

Associated do not include a fuel tank with their kits but recommend the Johnson tank for which their radio plate has a suitable slot to fit. This is of stout tinplate chicken hopper style, narrow and deep. Normal 'rat-race' quick filler fuel cap as standard. A very neat spring-loaded cap is on the U.S. market but not so far 'standard' for RC100.

SG have a tank peculiar to themselves, being of round section and made of brass painted black. I have heard that some of the paint gets inside and comes off with the fuel — certainly the paint wears off and shows the bare metal on the outside. With the earlier kits tank is angled to one side of the chassis; the latest Professional has it placed angled the other way. I don't know if there is any special significance in this.

PB offer a very neat pressure tank at a modest price which is easily assembled with the help of a little epoxy being of nylon in the main. This is a well tried accessory being common to the Expert series.

Radio Plates

We have already mentioned the important part the RC100 radio plate plays in mating the firm and flexible parts of the chassis. This is the only one that is significantly raised above the main chassis and cut out to take radio gear.

In the earlier Expert kits (still continuing of course) PB had a similar though lighter gauge plate enclosed in a U-shaped radio box which went round the fuel tank. This is lidded and latest thinking is that taking the lid off wastes time!

Hence current r/p hugs the chassis, for lower cg, being separated from it only by rubber cushioning grommets. Radio mounting posts are provided to carry radio on one side and battery on the other slung on stout rubber bands. Rear posts double, being taller as body shell mounting posts. Servo brackets are also provided.

SG follow a very similar procedure, with rather more elaborate servo brackets. Almost the only item where approach is identical!

Ancillary Equipment

Heatsinks, silencers (mufflers to American readers) and the like are not normally part of the kit, though purpose made units are available from the manufacturers.

The ordinary flat plate heatsink is giving place to the more elegant 'big head' type of replacement head for engines. It not only looks better but takes up less space. PB make a very smart unit, machined from the solid, worth every bit of the price charged for it. SG who work hand in hand with Super Tigre enjoy that company's diecast head which comes as part of the complete Super Tigre X21 engine. USA makers again offer a range of heads, though clinging more to the flat head style.

Silencers have assumed considerable importance in Europe with noise level regulations (more severe than in America). Designs now involve no power loss, indeed with pressure fed fuel tanks venting into the silencer, are of practical benefit and no longer necessary evils. The stand up round dustbin type is favoured by PB, and located on a platform just behind the engine. SG have been offering a conventional wrap round type, but are now moving towards a larger separately fitted design, if their latest exhaust extension piece means anything.

Bodies

Little need be said about bodies — or body shells, they seem to be regarded rather like bathing trunks as something which must be worn in public! Some of the finest

Below: Basic SG Futura III kit developed over a number of earlier models by designer Franco Sabattini and released at the 1978 German Toy Fair, when it was acclaimed by the experts.

Above: A late version of the PB International with MacGregor radio equipment installed. This has the earlier PB slide carb and simple trumpet air filter.

models are hidden by the scruffiest of bodies for most of the time: a best body coming out for finals. Keith Plested is trying to improve this image with a set of beautifully painted shells from his range to show what can be done. But a few meetings alas soon shows how unkind others are to bodies, which are involved in the most frightful pile-ups and come up unharmed, though battered. At the moment the best bodies moulded in Lexan come from America with prices somewhat on the high side. Perhaps a brave pioneer will start making similar quality shells in Britain with consequent saving.

Instructions

'When all else fails, read the instructions' used to be the cynical advice given to builders. In the cases of Associated and PB they really are worth reading, not only do they provide screw by screw details, but also a wealth of useful information on tuning, set-up and other whys and wherefores. Associated have the better pictures: PB will be following suit when pressure of production allows, at present clear diagrams and rather smudgy pictures. SG, whose kit is nearly RTR, offer no instructions at all.

What Should You Buy?

Financially the price range is from £75 for PB International to £69 for SG Futura III with Associated RC100 on offer at £80. Not an entirely comparative choice since the included items vary slightly — a Johnson tank for the RC100 may cost nearly £12 in the U.K. Prices will also vary according to country. Cheaper nearer home of course.

The experienced driver will already have strong views on what he needs and likes, and be hard to wean from successful equipment. The newcomer will be wise to follow local choice since he can draw on the help of others with similar equipment in the club or vicinity. Style of racing will also influence choice. The greater traction of American tracks would seem to favour the Associated range, though their successes in 1977 at the European Championships might appear to contradict this 'horses for courses', until we remember that Lyon-Lentilly is a very good traction circuit (and hard on tyres).

On the other hand the recently (first season) PB International has had an outstanding season at home, clocking up an almost 100% victory roll on major U.K. Open Meetings. With an excellent continental coverage, we can expect a great deal more from the marque in 1978; indeed if qualifying times are studied it is already way ahead of most competitors. SG naturally has a specially strong following in its native Italy. Ideally matched with the Super Tigre it has been getting high placements, particularly in the hands of flexy chassis specialists. With recent improvements to the preferred engine it can be even more formidable.

The most general all round kit must be the PB International. You may never be good enough, or a clever enough tuner, to win many races with anything, but you will probably get the most and soonest pleasure straight from the box with it, and certainly the least grief in learning to drive. For the man who likes the building up of the kit, and wants to put in his own little refinements, then the Associated RC100 would be his ultimate choice. He can start with the stark simplicity of the RC2, and add bits gradually to produce the RC100 when he is capable of handling it. It is really a matter of the driver who wants to enjoy working on improvements as well as racing versus the man who wants to race and never mind why it goes as long as it goes. You can pick out both sorts at any meeting!

Right: Super Tigre X21 engine and SG silencer a combination that has always been a successful partnership.

11: Associated RC 100

With a Little Help from the New RC200

HARDLY HAD I sat down to rough out this piece than news arrived of the RC200 a vastly improved version to make all other marques out of date, or so I though until I had the good fortune to see the advance copy en route to the Nuremberg Toy Fair. Splendid it certainly is, and a future joy and pleasure to many, but, in keeping with the established Associated system, all marques modify upwards or downwards. Briefly, the additions include fibreglass chassis, new front end to provide full Ackerman steering, improved spring-loaded filler cap to tank, thicker rear axle. Any one or all of these mods can be added to existing RC100s. I did not mention disc brake since this is already an RC100 option.

Starting to Make up the Kit

Instructions are splendid as supplied. I will elaborate on matters which presented some difficulty, or where instructions could have been more detailed. Order of assembly is straightforward: Power pod; motor mounts; brake; clutch; engine; radio; fule tank mounting; chassis assembly; front end; servo saver; front bumper; rear/wheels; linkage. This involves quite a bit of jumping about from one end to the other and I preferred to finish off the power pod unit entirely before looking elsewhere, apart from checking that I had all the bits!

Power Pod

Holes are drilled or cut out to locate axle bearing blocks, clutch bellhousing and engine crankcase, with slots to take motor mount bolts, allowing some movement for

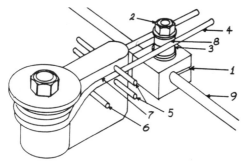

Left: Ball bearing tie rod assembly. 1. Aluminium block for tie rod. 2. Mounting screw. 3. Two flanged ballbearings. 4. Heavy duty servo saver spring. 5. Piano wire locating pins for servo saver spring. 6. Pin to keep servo saver upright. 7. Spring arms to rest against plastic. 8. .003 clearance where spring arms abut. 9. Tie rod goes into ball ends to provide 5° toe in.

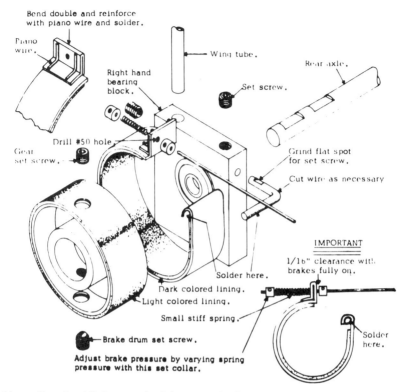

Bend double and reinforce
with piano wire and solder.

Piano wire.

Wing tube.

Rear axle.

Right hand
bearing
block.

Set screw.

Drill #50 hole.

Gear
set screw.

Grind flat spot
for set screw.

Cut wire as necessary

IMPORTANT

1/16" clearance with
brakes fully on.

Solder here.

Dark colored lining.

Light colored lining.

Small stiff spring.

Solder
here.

Brake drum set screw.

Adjust brake pressure by varying spring
pressure with this set collar.

Above: Details of fitting standard drum type brake.

different gear ratios. Mounts are drilled to take the Veco 19, though this is unlikely to be the usual propellant for most people aspiring to the RC100. However, other engines can, as the book says, be easily mounted by either drilling new holes in the motor mounts, or slotting the holes in the engine itself. The latter course should be avoided if possible since there is seldom a great deal of spare material to allow much more than a little enlargement of holes by reaming out.

Three other lightening holes are also to be found on the power pod. A trial assembly of wheels and axle can be made since tyres are happily already bonded onto wheels. This leads to next step, sorting out the standard brakes. A separate instruction sheet is provided for this, which might lead one to suppose is a trifling little job to be done in a tick. Not so; there is first of all the tricky business of the thick steel wire to which the brake band is attached. There is plenty of wire and the greater part must be cut off as superfluous. Some trial and error assembly is needed.

Anything to do with soldering that must be firm I view with respect, and try to make up a jig so that the work is held exactly where I want it and I have only to wield the iron. Here the brake band is to be approximately $\frac{1}{4}$ in larger in diameter than brake drum so a piece of scrap wood is cut out to this size in which the band rests snugly. It is drilled and cut so that the wire right angle fixing to the axle bearing block can be located rigidly. Other end of band is bent over as instructed after being rubbed with emery and painted with solder paint (I use Fryolux but there are undoubtedly other good makes throughout the world). A part of the jig is cut away here to give access to this end.

For soldering piano wire I invariably use Baker's Fluid an acid flux which is ideal for steel (never use it of course for electrical joints!) Since it is acid thoprough washing in water afterwards is necessary. Wire end to go into motor mount can be trimmed to size, but leave enough of the other end for handling purposes, marking with a file cut where it will end in the piece of bent over brake band. File or saw off flush, only after fixing. A good sturdy bit with plenty of heat and a fairly high melting point solder are needed. Repeat HOT IRON — the secret of soldering. Get it firmly fixed. If not satisfied, heat, unsolder and do it again. Failure here will be likely to tangle up the car during a race. Clean metal bright and shiny, acid flux, hot iron and a strong job results. If you make no claim to be a solder king, do try with a bit odd bits and pieces to acquire the knack. Like riding a bicycle the knack will come suddenly and you're laughing.

For other end a little blow torch flame will melt the solder paint. For the lighter gauge piano wire reinforcement about 20 swg will do, bind in place with fuse wire and touch with hot bit using quite safely here a normal cored solder. Remove any bits of fuse wire, and rub down. Final job here is to drill for the brake push/pull rod. Stick the two linings and assemble. After all this palaver, many builders will opt for the disc brake option. It is easier to fit and in common with most views, is I believe better (some motorcyclists may not agree!).

After this fitting clutch, another separate sheet, will be child's play. Do not drop the split-spring pins — now slightly bigger than they used to be — and press them in with a bench vice as recommended. Gently does it! Whether you follow the new mode of metal to metal or decide to line the clutch bell depends on the sort of speeds you expect to attain and the engine you fit.

Below: End product! This is Al Chuck's Concours Winner at the Pomona World Championships.

Chassis

Some power pods have a recess ground to accept the chassis plate. I have one like this and one without a recess that looks to be an earlier model. Anyway pod goes on top of plate and is duly secured with three nuts and bolts. This would be the end of it but for the plastic radio mounting tray. Originally you had to cut this out to shape, now it comes with cut outs for fuel tank, battery and receiver, leaving only the servo cutouts to make to suit your servos. The two outer securing bolts attaching pod to chassis plate are in fact long bolts on which the radio tray is secured, as per the book. A third bolt at the front of the plate and through the chassis completes the fixing with the proviso that instead of being firmly fixed at the front, a metal washer allows a degree of play to enable the chassis to flex. It all seems a little complicated but is easier in the doing.
take in front end heading

Above: This is bare RC100, shown here with an earlier and simpler fail-safe connection to track rod. Radio plate and connections included in kit but not shown here.

Right: Disc brake unit now offered as an option. Can be very accurately adjusted for braking effect.

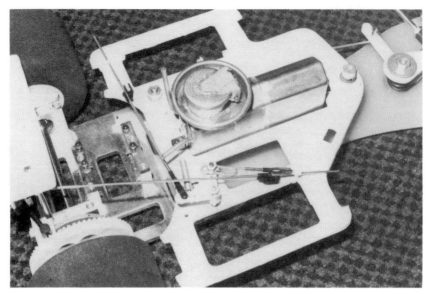

Above: Radio plate installed and cut out to take the Johnson tank with fliptop tank top. Plate is not normally supplied cut out with the RC100.

Front End

Originally a pair of front cross arms were assembled with the steering blocks and stub axles and then adjusted to be true and twist free. Now a splendid machined alloy cross piece is available into which the steering blocks/stubaxle assemblies are fitted. These items are the only remaining thing that could usefully be improved by a single piece casting, nylon moulding or machined unit from the solid (I hope to find time to do it for mine before the season opens).

The steering servo has now been improved in company with the front track rod. The latter now slides through a split block and is secured centrally. Ball jointed ends connecting with the steering arms. A double ballbearing unit rides on the split block and the servo saver arms are located and set between two wires through the plastic and rest against the ballbearings, thus ensuring the sweetest possible steering movement. But, stop! The latest RC200 goes a step further with a radically altered (though still a family likeness) servo saver, plus a pair of Delta(?) tie rods to the balljointed ends. Altogether a much more attractive picture and strongly recommended to the man who enjoys a workmanlike and efficient set-up. To what extent it is more effective than before remains to be seen, but it certainly looks good.

Build in tow-in to suit. Gene Husting is a great one for toe-in and sometimes frightens even his friends — but go at least half to three quarters of the way he suggests, you may go the last bit when you see how it works.

Linkages

Sketches provided make these very clear — far more than words could. Very little changes will be required if disc brake is fitted, since there is still a push/pull action.

Some mods may be necessary if any of the more sophisticated carbs, such as the Thorp are used. Certainly in this case fit a little bracket to take the auxiliary high speed needle valve rather than leaving it floating free on a fuel lead as I saw a few weeks ago!

The Oddments

Front and rear body mounts, bumper plate and follow the customary pattern. Choice of heat sink depends very much on personal preference. The 'big heads' are for the most part still being hand machined and quite costly. Associated offer an attractive and different combined head style like the slip-on rectangular heat sinks but combining a head; Super Tigre include theirs with the engine. Probably other will do the same in the future.

Silencing again is a matter of choice. I would not look further than the 'dustbin' offered by PB and Ted Longshaw in several varieties. If fitted in a stand-up position a little extension platform cum rear bumper is worth fitting and neatens off that end as well as strengthens it (This is where you are most likely to be getting the knocks — always assuming you are ahead at some stage of the race!).

Final thought! Nuts that are likely to be nearly permanent fixtures during the life of the car could well be secured with a drop of Loctite.

Below: Latest fail safe servo saver on RC200, adjustable track rods and fully machined cross-beam.

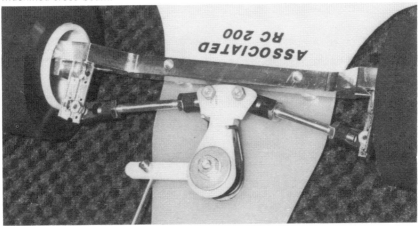

12: Doing the Delta

'THE CAMPBELLS' have been in the r/c model car game — business? — almost since the beginning, their first catalogue appeared in 1969, and they can justly claim to be the oldest firm still going strong (one earlier firm has not lasted). Ken plus wife Gloria and Ken's brother Bill form the triumvirate, hence 'Delta' the greek D forming a triangle. But we must not forget that other Delta 'great' who have been driving their cars to victories over the years none other than Art Carbonnel, a legend in his lifetime!

I was therefore specially pleased to hear from Bill, who is the research and products side with details of the company. Looking at the kit drawings provoked an immediate desire to try out a car since not many seem to be operating in Britain — largely I feel because much of the company's publicity is strictly word of mouth. Sight of the 760JL provided by Ted Longshaw confirmed early interest so here we are.

What a Difference

Like other successful American kits Delta have followed a policy of steady improvement over the years, adding, improving or changing parts only as better could be evolved, and race testing had confirmed their views. Many accessories now in general use first had an airing in prototype form in a Delta car . . . so that some parts give one a strange feeling of deja vue.

Chassis plate is a single alloy plate the full length of the car. Strength and rigidity is given to the rear end by bolting on two beautifully machined side bearers described respectively as clutch hanger and engine hanger. This introduces a major difference.

Below left: Shaping a tyre fast on the lathe using a hacksaw blade. Cover rest of lathe with a sheet – it's filthy black dust everywhere. Below right: Simple mandrels turned up in a few minutes from bar. Worth making; they last until you lose them.

Above: The very latest 1978 Super J Delta on the famous Delta 'tweak table'. Still basically the 76OJL (now re-named Panther) I have made until you discover the numerous refinements. The beautifully machined hangers supporting engine on near side and ball-bearinged clutch support on the far side. Note also ball-bearinged axle bearings and additional bar for rigidity.

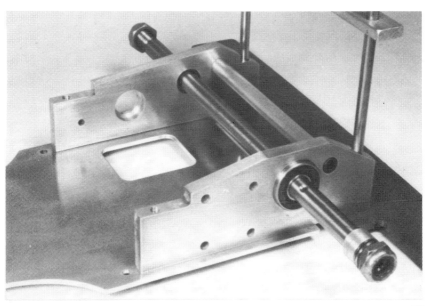

Above: Items lined up to assemble clutch, bellhousing and gear on crankshaft.

Recommended engine Veco 19 is **not** supported on conventional engine bearers but bolted to engine hanger through the holes retaining the engine endplate. These holes must be carefully drilled and tapped out (using NC 4-40 taper and 2nd tap; obtainable if you do not already have them from any good tool shop). Indeed, to digress, anyone using any amount of American gear should have the more common tap and drill sizes in NC thread to take $\frac{5}{8}$ in cap screws which are longer than those retaining the engine backplate. At the same time two or three thin washers are introduced to permit some manoeuvring space for clutch bellhousing end float (about 015-030).

This is not the only surprise. Veco crankshaft must be shortened so that it is $\frac{11}{16}$ in in length measuring from the bearing. The Veco tapered collet is slid off to take this measurement. The shortening can be best done by grinding off, taking care not to overdo it. At this stage the clutch parts can be examined and a trial set up made with the two hangers in place to see just what is being attempted. I do hope that all this so far is being done with plan laid out in front of you and the kit bits spread out for identification. Design of flywheel and flyweights differs again from common practice — just another little surprise! But it is not finished yet — and this is to my mind one of the nicest differences, the crankshaft is supported by the clutch hanger. That is to say we have overcome the system by which only one end of the shaft is held — we have both ends held which must surely be a better engineering answer than any other. Always provided, of course that the whole mounting is perfectly rigid. This explains the reason for the two side hangers. They are stout and hold that rear end vicelike, whilst still allowing enough frontal flex for the steering end.

With the aid of the little washers between engine hanger and end plate of Veco 19 some modest degree of endfloat can be arranged for the clutch bellhousing. It only needs a very little — but that little is really desirable. Once the general set up is grasped then the crankshaft can be ground down as required with every confidence.

Below right: First stage of fitting clutch shoes. Below left: Clutch shoes both nicely tucked in.

Above left: Clutch parts laid with machine vice for fitting. Above right: Adjusting end float for bellhousing with a feeler gauge. Adjustment washer can be seen on right. Two were needed.

Rear axle and clutch bearings are fitted in place and secured with Loctite. Note also the rear hanger spacer which ensures the rigid fitting of this end. Take a look at the neat brake arm. A little quiet relaxation at this stage would be to bond on the brake and clutch linings and also the tyres to the wheel hubs. Delta recommend the pregluing of hubs and tyres and then tipping lacquer thinners. More usual is the customary spreading of Evo-stik and pushing into place without delay. This is very much a matter of personal choice. I am an Evo-stik man and follow Keith Plested's excellent method by fitting the hub on a mandrel in the lathe, turning the headstock by hand whilst sliding on the tyre. Sticky tyre is held in plastic envelope used as a glove mitten. This is non-frustrating and keeps the hands clean. Spin the tyre round via the mandrel so that it runs true and leave to set off.

Delta even offer a special mandrel as an accessory for this desirable operation, which is followed by a certain amount of tapering off of wheels with a sanding block. However, a mandrel is so easy to make up that it is hardly worth the trouble (and expense) of acquiring a readymade one from distant parts. It takes only about ten minutes to make up a pair for front and rear wheels and they will last for ages until you lose/lend them.

Dodging now to the front end the steering can be set up. The interesting ballbearing front wheels will already have been noticed and the ballbearings duly installed, but gently, pressing on the outer rim of the race. Bearings are shielded and there should be

Below left: Only just enough room for the wheels to turn – so watch it! Below right: First thought: Kavan carb with Delta filter, but awkward to arrange throttle movement.

Car assembled. Fuel tube connections not made to show Delta tank outlets. Thorp slide carb now fitted. Only just room for the dustbin silencer.

no trouble with dirt working in, but remember to keep them lightly oiled. Of course there is the problem of having spare sets of front wheels all complete with ballbearings. This can be made a little lighter in two ways. First by getting some surplus bearings if possible; then by limiting raceday stocks to two spare pairs; finally by having a set or two plain bearing practice wheels.

The steering crossbeam is a single piece, that is there is no upper and lower claw to hold the kingpin it rests snugly and happily on top of the beam. A short socket head cap screw acts as a steering stop each side. Clearance inside the wheel hubs is quite critical and can be adjusted by the location of the sleeves through which the kingpost runs. When all is well the wheels go round and round in utter silence — you will know when.

There remains the set-up of servos, etc on the radio plate. This is ready cut out to take Futabas or similar and a suitable upright fuel tank. The Johnson will go in though not designed for it. Better is the special Delta fuel tank for which the whole is designed. This really also involves acquisition of a Delta slide carb including a second needle valve and pressurised tank. However, I struck a period of slide carb famine (new PB not in production and Greeno ceased production) and had to choose between an ancient very Mark 1 PB, a more elaborate arrangement to use a normal Kavan carb or a Thorp slide for my Veco. Since the servo layout is in line on the radio plate with a push for 'brake on' and a pull for 'engine off' a slide carb offers the neatest answer. It is not quite the answer as I have had to block off main jet connection on fuel tank until I get the genuine Delta slide gear. Tank also has that nice spring loaded filler cap similar to the one shown on the latest SG Futura (that man Campbell thinks of all these things first!).

On/off radio switch is mounted to operate from under the plate — this is easier to switch off with the body on. There is only just room at the back for a dustbin type silencer to sit — perhaps a slightly deeper rear bumper would be a good thing but I used the whole of the part provided. It is also quite critical getting the silencer attached to engine with only enough room to get the fuel connection clear of the fixing screw.

76

*Above: Front end assembled. Note robust connections and unsupported kingpins.
Below: Latest type Delta by Eddie Van Nylen (Belgium) but with a great big pumper
carb so he went to some trouble to arrange suitable linkage. It looks complicated
but it went well.*

13: Something Differential

Phil Booth

THE PB International car has been available since 1976, and has been very successful in bringing performance and reliability to novices and experts alike. But as with all racing cars constant development is needed to keep them competitive.

At the World Championships in California in 1977 the British team were taking more than a passing interest in the other team's cars, looking for any item that could be of use to them. One particular item that caught my eye was John Thorp's automatic car equipped with a differential which to my mind should have been of little practical use on a high traction surface with wide sweeping turns, but as Britain has some very tight circuits, and rather a lot of damp days, I thought it might have something to offer and would certainly be worth a try in one of our cars.

What a Differential Does

John Thorp who runs the Pomona Raceway in California where the World Championships were held in 1977 introduced the first model car differential in 1973. This is what his handout said: 'Losing traction and power in tight turns? Excessive tyre wear from high speed cornering? ... To solve these problems Team Thorp has developed a working differential type rear axle. Simple enough to adapt to most cars and rugged enough to stand up to the demands of competition, the new Thorp differential virtually eliminates wheel spin for greatly improved handling. It consists of

Below: Engine installed showing the narrow side of the gear box. It is really a very tight fit to install.

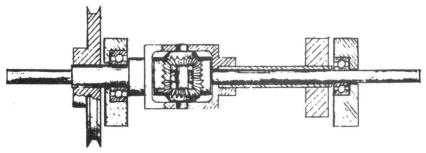

Above: Original Thorp diagram showing his differential – in his case operated by a belt drive from the engine.

a case, holding four bevel gears, two of which are fixed to half axles, and two idlers which mesh between the axle gears attached to the case. The case is driven by the gear through the axle tubes, with the force passing through the idlers to the axle gears. These idlers rotate to compensate any difference in the rotational speed of the axles.'

The *Dictionary of Technology* adds very little to this succinct description other than to say that the differential permits a rear axle to turn corners with one wheel rolling faster than the other, which is achieved by the faster turning wheel being balanced via the idlers by the slower wheel which lags by a like amount. In more advanced forms the amount of slip can be adjusted to a predetermined amount. In the model this is due to some degree by the nature of the oil used to lubricate the differential case. A fairly light engine oil for example at Mendip was just right, a thicker oil could alter the relative slip.

Two cars using the Thorp set up at Mendip driven by Phil Booth and Ted Longshaw also had even more of the 'Thorp package' by using HRE wheels which are standard to Thorp cars. These are rather more flexible than the solid PB wheels being spoked and had a degree of give which helped to spare the mechanism and improve roadholding.

Fitting

Unfortunately fitting the Thorp differential was not a straight-forward conversion,

Below: Slight cutaway on engine mount will be seen; also the oiling hole in gearbox.

Above: Thorp differential in place, with cover off to expose gears. Note the special wheel mounting to take flexible HRE wheels.

involving a lot of work and a change of rear wheels to the HRE type. Dave Preston drove this car at Tibshelf in a direct comparison with my standard car. The results were not very encouraging with apparently no noticeable advantage on either dry or damp parts of the track surface although we both thought the differential equipped car was possibly a little easier to drive.

Whilst I admit I was more than a little disappointed that the differential was not going to make me a World Champion overnight, the thought of chasing Dave Martin's exhaust smoke around the circuits for another year made me persevere for a little longer to make myself thoroughly familiar with its characteristics and try its behaviour on all types of surfaces, and enter some of the Winter series competitions to test its durability. Which brings me to the point of this chapter. It was at these meetings that many people, racers and spectators alike, showed great interest in the unit, as most questions were on, usually, the one subject 'What are its advantages if any'? Good question and not very easy to answer. I presume from the above question that most readers want to know what the results of the testing were, more than a long technical essay on how the thing works.

Suffice to say the differential allows the rear wheels to rotate at different speeds when negotiating corners, which should ease the load on the steering and make the car turn faster with less understeer. The biggest advantage to my mind after driving the car for many hours, is it is easier to drive, requiring less effort on the part of the driver to achieve good cornering lines and accurate positioning of the car. In fact any excess

Below left: The smaller spur-gear driven PB differential in prototype form. Below right: PB differential with engine in place. Its smaller size is a great help in assembly.

Above: This is the production model of the first British differential on the market made by AMPS and now adaptable to PB, SG, Associated and Serpent cars worldwide.

enthusiasm with the throttle stick only produces wheel-spin on the lighter loaded wheel, without affecting the directional stability of the car.

Unfortunately some difficulty has been experienced in achieving an acceptable braking performance with the single rear disc, which appears to favour locking one rear wheel when braking heavily into tight turns, against the lighter loaded wheel. On top of this one has to consider two other factors against its use. One is the added complication of two half-shafts (which bend easily) and four bevel gears, which add a wear and reliability factor to an otherwise trouble-free part of the car. The second point, a penalty which most people would not even consider important at all, is the unit adds approx 8 ozs to an already heavy car.

Keith Plested, who is always very eager to try an ideas which might benefit his products, has already designed and manufactured an excellent compact differential using spur gears in an aluminium casing, which fits the International car with no modifications at all and even uses standard wheels, but he would only manufacture it on a production basis if he felt the results in terms of increased performance were worth the costs involved.

To sum up, the tests so far have proved inconclusive against a standard car with drivers of comparable skill, and even John Thorp himself (with a few exceptions) has not prevented the almost total domination of most events by the solid axle cars.

Below: Production PB differential with spur gears. Uses nylon Plummer blocks and normal PB wheels so is easy to install in designed car the PB International. It is currently the cheapest on the market.

14: PB International

Phil Booth

BUILD A PB International Car from a kit! Now that's a novel idea! In $1\frac{1}{2}$ years of racing International cars I have never built a kit car. Having heard both praise and criticism of the kit I was about to find out for myself.

Reading through the very comprehensive instruction I assembled the rear axle first. The axle blocks themselves have been strengthened at the weakest point to prevent the breakages that occurred on the early cars. The tight fit of the bearings on the axle gave me a few problems but I cured this by rubbing down the axle with fine wet or dry paper until the bearings slid right up to the axle shoulder. This is very important to achieve the correct spacing of the rear axle.

Fitting the roll pins to the disc brake collar was easy enough but having done this the collar would not slide on the axle. The reason for this being, the wall thickness between the roll pin hole and the inside diameter of the collar is very thin and when the roll pins are pressed or tapped in they spread the aluminium collar slightly closing up the inside diameter. A few minutes work with a file soon put this right.

Before sliding the disc on to the axle I drilled a few holes in it because I feel this helps to clean the disc of any oil and grit when the brakes are applied. I have also seen slots filed in the discs for the same purpose.

Below: The completed PB International.

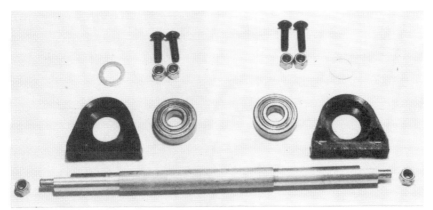

Above: Rear axle, ball bearings and axle blocks.

Two washers are provided to adjust the side float on the rear axle, but I could find no mention of these in the instructions.

For such a simple assembly the disc brake works very well provided it is assembled with a little care. Filing a radius on the operating cam provides a more progressive brake action, so a little bit of extra care on this is worthwhile; also make sure the brake pads slide easily on the $\frac{1}{16}$ in roll pins before fitting them to the caliper. Another point missing from the instructions is the necessity to file a flat on the operating cam for the brake arm grub screw to locate on to.

Before fitting the silencer to the rear chassis plate I knocked out the end caps and re-fitted them with silicone sealing compound, which helps to stop leaks. On this particular car the brake arm fouled the silencer and needed about $\frac{1}{8}$ in cutting off before it would clear.

Using the narrow chassis recommended in the instructions all the holes lined up perfectly and the assembly began to look like a car. The radio plate presented no problems but I think the stiffener plates might be better if they were wider, to enable

Below: Disc brake assembly and parts partially assembled.

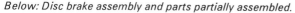

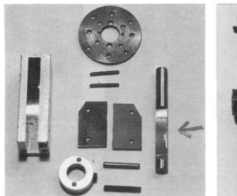

Above left: Disc brake parts laid out. Note holes drilled in disc. Above right: The failsafe-Ackerman-cum-servo-saver unit. A real blessing.

them to be formed into a L-section to make them more rigid.

The instructions should be followed carefully for the fuel tank assembly and if the tank is not drained after use and the ball valve wedged open the top plate will warp and gaps will appear between the screws. I believe Keith Plested is working on a new fuel tank design which should cure some of the problems and will also be a more adaptable shape.

Making up the servo saver is quite straightforward but I did find the pivot post was a rather tight fit in the nylon moulding, which made the operation rather stiff. Despite its strange appearance the push nut is a very secure way of keeping the tension of the spring and should never come loose.

Below: Rear axle fitted on power pod; wheels hubs on; rear bumper plate fixed and disc brake installed.

Above: Parts for the stub axle steering arm and kingpin assembly.

The front axle is quite a complicated assembly and I was pleased to find that all the parts went together with no problems at all, provided the components were carefully cleaned u and de-burred before fitting.

Even the axle end float was perfect, using the washers provided, but when fitting the track rod ball joints to the rod I thought the mouldings were a little loose on the threads, but this is a minor criticism.

The PB International clutch is unique in the use of a neoprene 'O' ring to control the shoes and with a little experiment on the weight of the clutch dhoes a very smooth action is possible. I have not heard of any problems resulting from the use of the 'O' ring.

The rest of the car is just a matter of fitting the bumpers and rear wing mounts, but I personally use an alloy front body mounting as an added safety factor having broken the plastic ones more than once.

In conclusion, I found the basic kit easy to assemble and very complete, and provided a little care is taken in the preparation of the components prior to fitting no trouble should be experienced. The finish of some of the parts leaves something to be desired when compared with some of its European and American competitors, but taking into consideration its price, which is cheaper than most of its rivals, the car itself has proved its race worthiness and durability beyond doubt.

I have never used the narrow chassis in competition, preferring instead to use the wide chassis suitably cut down and waisted to provide the necessary flexibility and I mount the receiver and Deac mounting posts directly to the chassis plate.

Below left: Broad and waisted chassis plate choice. An optional extra now is a GRP front chassis plate. Below right: Clutch assembled with O-ring.

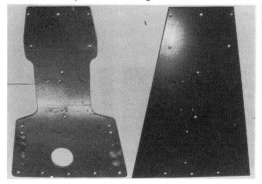

Above: Parts for the fuel tank. Build with meticulous care. A new tank design is now available.
Top left: Using the crankshaft adaptors to fit the O-ring on clutch shoes.
Left: The various parts for clutch, flywheel and bellhousing.

Another worthwhile modification is the independent brake adjuster, which is simple to make and provides brake adjustment at the turn of a screw. The nylon operating arm is free to rotate on the brake cam shaft and when the brakes are applied the arm comes into contact with the adjuster screw and operates the brake. The adjuster screw assembly is locked to the brake cam by a grub screw in the normal way.

15: Making Your Own Starter

'THE ONE thing most beginners ask is 'How do I make my own starter'.' This is a typical model shop's comment when invited to suggest a useful article for *Radio Control Model Cars*. So, here goes. Like Mrs. Beeton's famous hare, first get the starter motor; which should be the 12-volt kind.

Wearing old clothes, and with a few hefty tools in the boot, go along to the nearest car dump and seek out the man there. He will almost certainly be able to provide one and will charge anything from a mere 50p to £3. If possible also get the starter switch-on button, which in the case of an oldish motor will probably have the starting solenoid integral with it. Later models, since they have been operated by the on/off key on the steering column do not have a springloaded on/off switch like this. In which case you will need a solenoid. Lack of it will quickly pit contacts and is unsatisfactory. Maybe you will have to dismantle your starter with your own tools from the latest banger in ... hence the old clothes and tools ... but this should produce the cheapest product.

I expect your starter will have its throw-up gear still in place which operated the car flywheel. If you can persuade the man at the dump to remove it for you so much the

Below: Starter with trolley wheel erected on Dexion framework. This gives excellent earthing properties. With wooden framework be sure earth connections of common negative are good.

On/off bell-push (spring loaded)

Lighter twin-flex

Ex-car accumulator (or even new)

Ignore this connection

Solenoid

Ex-car starter motor

12v. battery

Common   negative

STARTER CIRCUIT (Not to scale)   Stout covered leads

Above: Starter circuit which should make connecting up clear. Some parts acquired may not be exactly like these but should be like enough to follow wiring.

better. If not you will have to get it off yourself. If you cannot get it off easily then you will have to saw off a small shaft end to free it. Just behind the retaining circlip the metal will probably not be hardened and will accept a hacksaw cut. Once this is off then a suitable hardened rubber wheel must be fitted.

Wheels used are generally off industrial trolleys and may not be easily obtained as a one-off. However, most model shops catering for r/c cars now carry a stock. A 4 in diameter wheel (ours is a Flexello) will cost between £1.25 and £1.50. Hole in wheel may have to be drilled or filed out a bit to go on shaft. It can be locked in place with a couple of allen screws if the hard rubber or plastic hub is tapped or shaft end tapped. Alternatively, you can try your luck sticking it with Loctite which seems to work marvels of adhesion . . . especially when you want to loosen a bolt . . . mine is Loctite-ed.

You will also need a spring loaded on/off button — you can use a bellpush from Woolworth's, or just look at one and see how simple it is to make up from a bit of springy brass or steel. Add to this a yard or two of stout electric cable, and a similar amount of lighter weight cable, and a pair of bulldog clips. Finally you need a 12 volt car battery. This is the most expensive part and may set you back some £15. A motor cycle battery is a little cheaper and lighter but will not stand up to the use so well or so long. You can as a makeshift measure use jumper leads from the family car. This is common practice amongst American drivers but is a bit awkward if you cannot get your car near the pits, and have to feed in through the bonnet. With boot located battery it is simpler. I did see one man at Lilford Park in 1977 sitting very happily on his boot ledge and doing just that.

How you house the apparatus when made depends on your talents. If you happen to have some Dexion or Handy-angle, this is the quickest way to make up the starter. It is good also as a beginning since you will probably wish to alter the layout later, either to have it built into your tool/spares everything box, or just peeping through a slit in your pit table, and operated with a foot switch. The Dexion type is primarily for ground level operation. You may prefer to make the container/framework of wood. This can be simple and crude hinged to fold up into small space, or an elegant piece of equipment, such as that being operated by Wes Raynor of Mardave.

My solenoid is described as 'suits most Ford cars' and cost £3.24 (shocking price

Above: Simple German starter that clamps on the bench. Right: Keith Plested's starter box, cum tyre/wheel store, cum glowplug power source uses a photographic carrying case as base.

Below: This one uses a hand starter slightly modified, and also holds miscellaneous tools and accessories.

really, so try to get one at the dump). There will be two substantial bolts in the centre with washers beneath. They are the two ends of the solenoid which make a clicking sound as they operate (like the flashers in a car). There will also be a little flat spade like connector to which one end of your bell-push lead will connect. The other end connects to a solenoid bolt, together with the positive (+) lead to the battery. THe other solenoid bolt is connected to the positive of the starter motor. There will probably only be one possible threaded bolt connewction to the motor and this is it. Negative earths to the motor body and to the Dexion framework you have built. If you use a wooden framework then you will have to provide a stout earth wire back to the solenoid body. The solenoid should be bolted on to the framework, and again has a negative body. Battery negative (−) connection goes from negative post to common negative Dexion framework. With all connections make sure they are good and adequate with bare metal to metal contact.

Press button and motor will operate. You are in business!

Below: Elegant German starter in alloy which also uses a commercially available electric hand starter.

16: Electric Trainer

Barry Tingay

The Beginnings

FIRST CAR built was a present for young son to keep him happy at meetings. It so appealed to others that now there is a growing fleet of them! Just what does this ⅛th electric car have that appeals? It is quiet — so that a spot of practice on a local car park will not bring the neighbours down on you! — it is clean — so that the domestic side of the household is happy — it has a reverse, so that one-man training without marshals is so much simpler. It is not noticeably slower than the beginner can handle with glow plug power. It is the same size and style of the glow plug engined car and so robust enough to take its fair share of knocks. It is quickly prepared and can be put away without an elaborate clean-up. Disadvantages? Shortish run without re-charging (say 8/10 minutes) as against nearly twice this time without re-fuelling. Even this can be countered with a spare set of nicads readily changeable.

This first car was Mardave based — a good economy measure. Probably many would-be builders will have the bits and pieces of a car and need not purchase everything from the start. After the successful debut of Car No 1, my second was scratch-built using Mardave axles, with the addition of ballraced plummer blocks at rear and ballraced wheels at front. Some cleaning up of layout also took place. At least two other cars were also either built entirely, or watched over and advised upon when made by club members.

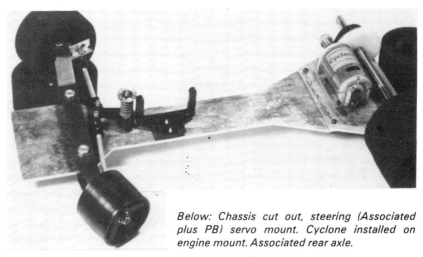

Below: Chassis cut out, steering (Associated plus PB) servo mount. Cyclone installed on engine mount. Associated rear axle.

Above: Prototype cars. Left is scratchbuilt No. 2; centre, Mardave improved; right, original No. 1 car.

Building the Trainer

Next step was to send for Ted Longshaw's catalogue and treat myself to an Associated Front Axle Kit (No 1210). When fitted to Car No 2 the handling was vastly improved. This decided me to build a completely new car as now described. Chassis is in two pieces, power pod and front chassis plate. Motor is Cyclone 15. In passing, when skill and ambition has been acquired, a simple change of power pod and you can be glow plug racing with the minimum of effort.

Chassis is made very stoutly from Aluminium Alloy HE15 TB $\frac{1}{8}$ in thick, 18 in long and $3\frac{1}{2}$ in wide. Cut off one end $4\frac{1}{4}$ in long, making due allowance for squaring the ends: this is the power pod. I used Spectra blue to aid marking out. Scribe centre line of rear axle and centre line of car. Mark out, centre punch, and drill the holes and the slot for gear clearance. I drilled $\frac{1}{8}$ in holes at each end and two between them, and sawed and filed the slot.

Deal with the front chassis plate in a similar way, squaring one end and marking out from there, coating with Spectra blue as before. Mark car centre line, and all holes to be drilled, working from rear squared end which will attach to pod. Front is left to last and cut off and squared at the very end. The $\frac{1}{8}$ in radii at the junction of the chassis waisting were made by drilling a pilot hole, and then drilling out with a $\frac{1}{4}$ in diameter counter bore. Chassis was then sawn and filed to shape.

Below left: Front chassis marked out and radii drilled ready for cutting to shape. Below right: Engine pod with motor bracket and plummer blocks in place.

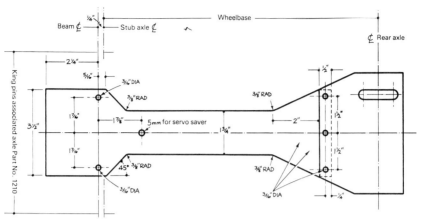

Above: Chassis front $\frac{1}{8}$ in by $3\frac{1}{2}$ in Ally alloy HE15. Fit bumper to suit body.

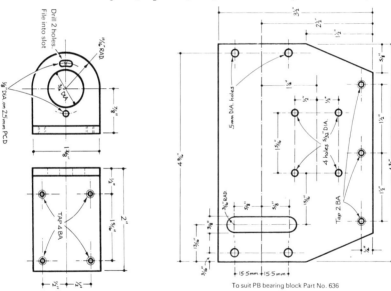

To suit PB bearing block Part No. 636

Above: Motor mounting bracket from 2 in x 2 in x $\frac{1}{8}$ in Ally alloy Angle.

Above: Power pod $\frac{1}{8}$ in Ally alloy HE15 $3\frac{1}{2}$ in x $4\frac{3}{4}$ in.

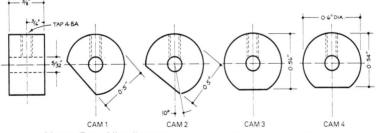

CAM 1   CAM 2   CAM 3   CAM 4

Above: Four Ally alloy cams, shown set in neutral position.

93

Motor bracket was made from a piece of 2 x 2 x $\frac{1}{8}$ in alloy angle. All the holes are marked out from the centre line, the $\frac{3}{4}$ in dia hole was again done with the counter bore. After all the holes were drilled and tapped motor was tried in place to check that it could be swivelled for final gear mesh adjustment.

Power pod is joined to chassis plate (pod on top) with 2BA button head or countersunk screws coming up from underneath. Two nuts go on the outer two screws, which also hold the radio plate, secured in turn with two more nuts.

Ballraces are pushed into their housings, with the races on the outside. The axle is located with the short turned end against the ballrace. The gear is then pushed out to the other ballrace so that when the bearing blocks are tightened there is no side movement. Screw down retaining grub screws to mark axle, then take down assembly and drill a dimple into which grub screws can locate. Re-assemble, tighten down, and adjust motor to correct gear mesh.

Front End

When fitting the steering cross arms, the lower unit should go under the chassis, the two spacers on top, then the upper cross arm. This will tilt the stub axles very slightly to provide a small amount of camber. If Associated wheels are used they go straight onto the stub axles. With PB wheels the stub axle bushes must be slightly shortened and rubbed down with fine emery to make a good running fit.

Switch Assembly

This may be new ground for many but requires only care and patience. Cut and drill the two side plates. They should be drilled together as a pair. Bending must provide opposite handed pieces, a left hand and right hand plate. To get the bends right, put them in the vice one at a time, and on top of the vice check with two pieces of $\frac{1}{4}$ in tool steel (or any similar true $\frac{1}{4}$ in material) that exactly a $\frac{1}{4}$ in is sticking up. Remove the measuring pieces and fold the flange over, using a block of wood and a hammer. If you have not done this sort of work before, practice with a bit of scrap sheet to get the hang of it.

Cams are from 0.6 in dia ally alloy rod, cut off $\frac{1}{8}$ in thick. Flats are filed exactly as shown on the drawing. Note that holes drilled and tapped for locating screws are all in the same relative position at neutral (as drawn). I have shown caphead screws holding them in place to make the photo clearer, allen screws do the job more unobtrusively, and are equally adjustable. These press down on the micro switches to provide the various speeds. With these parts made a trial assembly fit-up is next step, using two lengths of 6BA steel studding as shown.

When assembling switches slip 6BA studs through them; put mounting plates on loosely; fit nuts and slide shaft through into place. Stand mounting flanges on a flat surface (plate glass or similar) and tighten 6BA nuts. Remove shaft and put cams on in order, 1, 2, 3, 4. Lock cams 3 and 4 onto shaft so that the flats on them are parallel to each other. Turn the shaft until these two cams are horizontal, that is with the flats above the actuators of the micro switches. Turn cam 1 until the microswitch operates, then turn it a further 8 degrees approximately and lock into position. This is the neutral setting. Turn shaft a further 8 degrees (approx) and bring cam 2 round until it makes contact with its microswitch and lock in place.

Above left: Motor in place with gears in mesh. Above right: Microswitches and cams duly assembled.

Now when shaft is turned there should be three microswitch movements in either direction. Minor adjustments may be necessary. The sequence is:

1 down: 2 3 4 up = Neutral
1 2 down: 3 4 up = 1st speed
1 2 3 down: 4 up = 2nd speed
1 2 3 4 down = Top speed

For reverse direction the sequence follows, turning the other way:

1 2 3 4 up = Reverse 1st speed
1 2 4 up: 3 down = Reverse 2nd speed
1 2 up: 3 4 down = Reverse Top Speed

These switches switch a 1 ohm 25 watt resistor into circuit for 1st speed: 2nd speed switches a further 1 ohm 25 watt resistor into a parallel circuit: top speed switches a bypass lead in parallel with the resistors. Note that switching in parallel halves the value of any one resistor. In our case resistance becomes $\frac{1}{2}$ ohm. Resistors should be fixed to the chassis to assist heat dissipation.

Switch assembly operating lever can be filed up as shown from a scrap of alloy bar, or much simpler an old 13 amp earth pin from a fused plug is almost the exact shape required. About 30 degrees each side of neutral is movement required from the usual servo set-up. If when set up car goes the wrong way, then reverse polarity by changing over motor leads.

Gear Ratio and Fitting

The spur gear fitted to the motor is 16 teeth 32 DP. It requires to be opened up to $\frac{1}{4}$ in dia bore so that it can be fitted to the Cyclone 15 propeller adapter supplied in the motor kit. In the same way the 64T 32DP Delrin axle gear must be opened up to 10 mm dia bore. Boss must be reduced to $\frac{3}{8}$ in dia back 0.1 in and holes for two 2BA grub screws drilled and tapped.

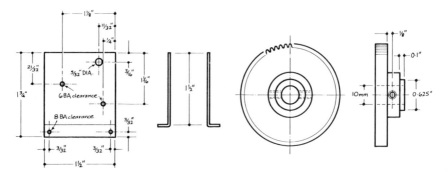

Above left: Microswitch/cam side plates. 2 off (left and right hand) 18 swg brass. Spindles 2 in x 5/32 in dia silver steel. Clamping studs 1-13/16 in x 6BA steel studding. Above right: Modifications to 64-teeth 32DP spur gear. Modification to 16T gear: Open up bore to $\frac{1}{4}$ in diameter

Battery pack should be installed as far to the rear of the main chassis plate as possible to keep weight well back.

Finishing the Trainer

This covers the parts which can either be made up easily, or that can be bought ready made and assembled. Body fixing, details of radio plate and the like will be very much the personal preference of the builder.

Parts List

Proprietary parts used or recommended are listed below. Some suppliers have minimum orders which may prohibit lone hands from buying though not club groups and in some instances trade supplies only available. To help such people *Radio Control Model Cars* has prepared a list available for SAE of items which the publishers will supply. Some work can also be carried out boring out gears, making up mount for motor, bearing plates and so on for those unable to complete their own.

Below: Wiring diagram for microswitches/motor.

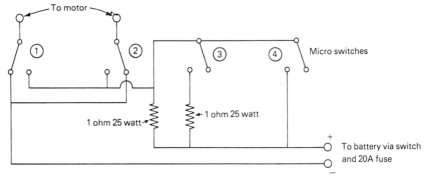

1 off PB Rear axle kit — Part No 686   1 off PB Servo saver — Part No 683
1 off PB Track rod kit — Part No 685   1 off PB Front hub kit — Part No 694
1 off PB Rear hub kit — Part No 693
1 off Associated RC1 Front End kit — Part No 1210. (above from Tom Longshaw's catalogue 50p returnable on purchase).
1 off Aluminium alloy HE15 TB 18 in x $3\frac{1}{2}$ in x $\frac{1}{8}$ in
1 off Aluminium alloy angle 2 in x 2 in x $\frac{1}{8}$ in x $1\frac{1}{2}$ in
2 off Brass sheet 18 swg $1\frac{3}{4}$ in x $1\frac{1}{2}$ in
1 off *Aluminium Alloy HE15 bar 2 in x 6 in dia
*(NB — size and material not critical, though if dia changed mounting plate must be re-drawn) (from J. Smith & Son Ltd, Biggleswade)
1 off 64 teeth 32 DP Delrin spur gear   1 off 16 teeth 32 DP steel spur gear
(above from S. H. Muffett Ltd, Tunbridge Wells)
4 off V3 Microswitches, Part No 337 — 857
2 off 25 watt wirewound 1 ohm resistors Part No 157 — 522
(above from R. S. Components — Trade supplies only)
1 off Ripmax Cyclone 15 kit (includes motor, propeller adapter, harness, switch, charge led and 8 cell 1.2 amp Nicad battery pack (above from most good model shops).

Below: Cams, switch brackets, microswitches, etc. One side plate shown unbent.

17: Building the Puma Stock Car   Paul Dudley

CHASSIS AND running gear come ready assembled. Very little additional work is required on the chassis itself as it is already plated and front bumper has been strengthened. Two body styles are available, standard and coupe; they are self coloured and available in six different colours. Material is glass fibre which makes for robustness.

Clutch and Engine Installation

Car illustrated has a Super Tigre installed, but any engine can be fitted including HB, Veco, Enya, Webra, OS, Fuji. First step is to assemble clutch and flywheel to the engine. This is fairly simple but care must be taken to get the clutch shoes the right way round — pivot point must be on the leading edge of the shoe. The all steel (note no clutch lining) needle bearing bellhousing is slipped on the shaft and fixed in place with the washer and screw provided.

Engine is then mounted on the slotted mounting plates. If care is taken at this stage it is possible to mount the engine with sufficient space between the end of the engine shaft and the chassis to enable the drive belt to be changed without removing the engine once installed. With the plates now on the engine, place in the car with the steel spacers between the mounting plates and the chassis. Before the engine is bolted down it is

Below: The Puma kit as it comes from the box.

98

Above: Parts of clutch and bellhousing laid out.

strongly advised that some form of bedding down material is placed between the mounting plates and chassis. This can take the form of liquid silicone or Isopon body filler. While it is in a semi-soft state the mounting plate and bolts are just finger-tight, only being tightened up properly when hard. This ensures a perfect vibration-free mounting.

Drive Belt

The drive belt can now be placed on to the clutch drive gear and the rear nylon drive gear, leaving about $\frac{1}{4}$ in play in the belt. It will be noted that there is already a flange on the nylon drive gear to stop the belt slipping off. Line up the drive gear with the clutch drum gear.

Engine Accessories

A heat sink should be attached to the cylinder head. Super Tigre engine comes with one already, others do not. These are quite inexpensive and can be secured with a single tightening screw. A suitable silencer exhaust must also be fitted to comply with noise regulations of not more than 80dB at 8 metres.

Tyres

Tyres are fitted to hubs in the usual manner with Evo-stik or similar adhesive, not neglecting to rough up the rims with sandpaper to secure good adhesion. It is a useful tip on performance on the oval stock car circuit to achieve controlled understeer, which

Below left: Steering block and kingpin springing. Note welded on crossbeam.
Below right: Front end showing steering and failsafe. Note ball joints.

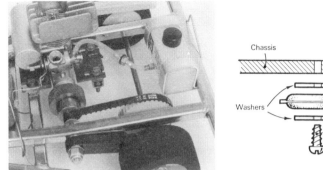
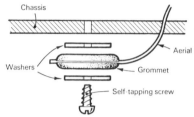

Above left: Engine, fuel tank, rear springing and belting. Above right: Aerial attachment for whip type aerial.

can be obtained by using extremely hard front tyres, or by getting the inside front wheel to lift when cornering.

Fuel Tank

Mount the fuel tank by fitting the aluminium straps provided around it and securing them underneath the rear bumper with the small self tapping screws. Connect tank to engine with a short length of fuel tubing, not forgetting to fit a fuel filter.

Radio

Radio box is mounted on the chassis plate with 4BA bolts provided. Installation shown is a typical Futaba layout, incorporating Micro Mold servo saver and balljoints.

Below: Paul Dudley's stock car painted up in sponsor's livery (Paul is a printer!).

Other equipment is equally satisfactory: only 'must' is the servo saver. Servos are generally installed using double-sided servo tape. Deac should be fixed to chassis through radio plate box with strap supplied, that is in same way as tank fixed. Receiver should be well packed in foam. S slot is cut in box lid to take the switch harness. Throttle linkage again is a matter of personal preference; it can be either a direct system or via a bellcrank incorporating a hand throttle. This leaves only aerial to be attached to the chassis. I recommend a piano wire whip, well insulated from the chassis, using a rubber grommet as shown in the sketch. Then wind aerial round the whip and secure at the top with short length of silicone tubing.

The Body

As stated the body — in choice of colours — is of glass fibre. This makes cutting out of the windows a little more difficult. The best method is to mark out shape required and then go round with a small drill until centre can be removed. Clean up rough edges with a half-round file and decorate to choice, using Humbrol enamel as there is then no need to fuel proof it.

Final Remarks

Although the most expensive stock car kit on the market, there are a number of exclusive refinements and excellent overall performance to make it well worth the extra cost.

18: The Body Beautiful

IN THE hurly burly of racing miniature cars the greatest all time sufferer is the car body which is often driven over, rolled over, scratched in a muddy gritty outfield or otherwise abused. For that reason it was very necessary at the outset of competitive racing to produce bodies that would not only last out the race but continue to give service for some appreciable time.

Elegantly built bodies in beaten metal or elaborately finished and painted in balsa wood that had graced some of the fast running cable cars in the immediate postwar period were definitely out. One such survivor will have been seen at Pontins first Model Week at Brean Sands when Jim Batten a veteran of those days brought along his car suitably modified for r/c operation. It excited wonder but no desire for emulation in its polished dural racing body that represented many hours of patient panel bashing.

The answer for car drivers was to be found in vacuum formed bodies of a variety of materials. Not the hard and often brittle plastic that takes such magnificent detail for highly finished nonworking models — though even here some of the more recent products can take an immense amount of hard usage — but the softer more yielding materials such as Butyrate and Lexan. Using male moulds enabled these to be produced quickly and economically in respect of Butyrate though naturally at the expense of

Below: This shows what can be done with a simple ABS bodyshell with little more than lining and some transfers, plus a supply of Letraset. This was decorated by Dave Wragg, reigning stock car champion.

Above: A Parma Lexan/Brabham body painted up and lined with a few transfers or decals. Parma are the largest supplier of Lexan bodies and hail from USA.

detail. However, since cars would mainly be seen at some distance and at speed a 'stand-off' scale appearance was the accepted thing.

The Butyrate moulds are usually offered in white at very reasonable prices and in a good variety of body shapes representing most of the fullsize racing cars in the public eye. Indeed, as soon as some new make achieves fullsize fame there will be replicas in $\frac{1}{8}$th and 1/12th scales as fast as photos can be studied and a quick mould made up. These moulds can be painted up using aerosol cellulose paints from motor accessory shops and are a quick way to get a cover on an otherwise complete racing machine. Other materials of a similar nature are also used including some in various primary colours.

The bodyshells, as they are called, require to have excess material cut away and the wheel arches cut out. This can be done either with sharp scissors, a fret saw or a hot iron. The last named tends to be rather smelly. Appropriate openings must be cut for access to controls and to give room for heatsink and glow plug access. It is a racing mandatory requirement that 'drivers' shall be seated in cars. These are very often moulded in with the body and simply require painting. Others have drivers as a separate moulding, which is rather better and allows for more freedom in arranging the layout.

Preliminary Work

Until recently a Lexan bodyshell was very much of a luxury, but with the recent introduction of home produced shells the price has come much closer to the ABS type body. Range is still fairly limited, and recourse to the wider range of American imports is necessary if an exotic body shape is demanded. There is also the range of ready painted bodies, again for money plus, to satisfy the ultra lazy or hamfisted driver.

It is usual to have both Sports/GT and Formula bodies to use on the same chassis with a minimum of alteration, perhaps, hopefully little more than a different pair of bumpers and retaining posts. Some compatibility of size should be looked for in making a choice.

Bodies all come with the sheet edges still sticking out all round. These must be cut away. With Butrate bodies the choice is between cutting with scissors or with a hot iron

103

Above: The unlucky Tyrrell six-wheeler decorated in blue and white and concealing a 1/12th scale Mardave electric car suitably altered to handle the four wheel steering.

(very smelly). Lexan is tougher and the ideal cutting implement is a good pair of tin snips. Look your body over and check that there are clear indentations where wheel arches come and where the body ends. Some may be very vague so mark them in on the outside of the shell in a chinagraph pencil line (it can be wiped away afterwards if any remains). Finish the edges with sandpaper to get it good and smooth. It pays to make up also a small round sander out of, say, an old boot-polish tin with the bolt through it with a strip of glass paper stuck round the edges. This is a round way of finishing wheel arches when mounted in an electric drill.

Just to be very obvious: the paint goes on the **inside** of the shell! To get good adhesion rough up the surface with a little steel wool, taking care **not** to touch any windscreen openings or the like where simulated glass finish is required. These areas had better be masked off early on. The Sellotape brown parcel tape of a Melanin base is good for this though it is quite expensive to buy as a roll. Failing this I have a fondness for the old fashioned brown paper sticky tape, which should be thoroughly wetted before putting on. The modern stuff does not seem to stick like it used to and it may be necessary to add some flour paste to get a real good stick. It washes off in warm water afterwards. Always check that edges of any masking such as this is as firmly fixed as possible. If you are masking off large areas tape edges only then fill in the bigger areas with newspaper or similar — saves tape.

While the shell is still clear slip over your car and see where the cut-outs will have to come. Use the faithful chinagraph pencil to mark them in. Cut out with a drill hole first, then slip a fretsaw blade through and cut round. It can be done with a knife blade but is more liable to slip. Wrap a piece of sandpaper round a pencil to finish off openings for things like fuel filler.

The Painting

Well what colours are you going to use and why? Don't be obvious! One heat in British GP attracted six cars all in red basic with white stripes — a timekeeper's nightmare, let alone a driver's! Colouring, apart from looking pretty, is mainly to enable the driver to pick out his car at a distance, his pit men to snatch it in for refuelling, and generally for supporters to be encouraging the right car. Another and more profitable use is for sponsor's colours and name to be imprinted thereon, but do keep in mind the primary need is to be able to see it. Dark green for example (although traditionally the old British Racing Green) is hard to see against a grass shoulder on the far side. Yellow is good colour, so is orange, and even some of the dayglo colours if you can get good ones.

White is a wonderful standby base colour and continues to be very popular. Butyrate cars usually come in this colour anyway so early laziness is impressed on one. Blue, certainly light blue, does not photograph well in black and white, so camera conscious drivers should beware. Dark blue is splendid, and also that middle blue sometimes called Rolls Royce Blue, but any pattern should be enlivened by stripes of one sort or another. Fashion seems to be to run them lengthwise on the car. I prefer transverse stripes, good and broad at the nose end of the car. Easy to see and quick to distinguish which way the thing is pointing.

When all else fails look at *Motor Sport* colour section for ideas — but remember you have got to do the work so make it fairly simple. True scale finishes — John Player Lotus in black and silver for example — look beautiful when fresh, but oh, the grief when it rolls over and over!

Make a sketch of your proposed scheme in colour (colour biros) and then cut out the masking in bits. This can be done on a sheet of glass — failing a better piece lay it out on a good big window, which is quite practical if self adhesive tape is used. Otherwise on a glass coffee table if non sticky masking is use. Shapes can be cut with a pointed modelling knife, using a coin for curved parts, or a cup, or a glass bottom for guiding with bigger pieces.

The Paint

You can use the inevitable spray can from any motor accessory shop — I am just as guilty here as anyone — it is so simple quick and clear. It may chip off and will require fuel proofing but it meets an immediate need.

Stop! Do not use the ordinary aerosol cellulose spray on Lexan bodies! It is perfectly all right for Butyrate but will not prove compatible with Lexan. If you are in any doubt at all about the paint you are using on Lexan, if it is not specifically stated as suitable, do try it first on a piece of offcut from the trimming. **You have been warned!** In general enamels are usable and of course the paints intended for Lexan and so described. Some

Below: One of the beautiful bodies marketed by Graupner for their range of cars and supplied ready painted. This one is cut away rather more than is usual to expose the Graupner 'works'.

are also fuel-proof so do not need an after-treatment. They are quite expensive but worth the extra in the better finish obtained.

I also continue to use my old Humbrol Jet-Mix spray gun with refills, which may or may not always be on the market. If you are not yet committed it would pay to get a middle priced outfit such as the Badger air brush which will last for a long time and also serve to touch up the family car between times. Or you can use brush — coachbuilders did for hundreds of years. I have some cans of the special Lexan paint that Ted Longshaw sells. This is fuel proof so only requires one painting operation to complete. It has been specially mixed for the job with the necessary amount of plasticiser and pigmentations for solid colours. Only snag at the moment is the somewhat limited range of colours available. Also, imported from USA, is the **Perfect Paint** offered by Mick Charles Models, another fuel proof paint, again without any very bright colours since it is mainly intended for model aircraft use and scale models.

Either can be thinned with appropriate thinners and used with a gun. Better several light coats rather than one thick coat. Give the job a full twenty-four hours to dry thoroughly before testing the fuel proof quality, but peel off adhesive tape within half an hour: sticky tape leave on and wash off later.

Good Advice on the Paint Can

'Almost all drying problems are caused by: (1) Using the wrong thinner, (2) applying when too cold or too humid (apply paint at temperatures above 70 degrees), (3) resins under the paint not dry (allow 72 hours for any epoxy filler or other potential soluble to dry).

'If paint comes off when masking tape is removed it is because (1) the wrong thinner was used, (2) the surface was not properly sanded, (3) the paint was not dry.' Use good quality plastic tape.

Below: A host of ideas! Take your choice of paintwork from this section of a World Championship line-up from California.

19: The Contest Scene

RACING IS very much the name of the game, and over the years a number of racing patterns have been evolved. None are entirely satisfactory but on the whole no aspiring young driver need feel that there is no niche for him on the grounds of inexperience or lack of the means to compete with more expensively equipped opponents.

Outdoor racing on permanent purpose-built circuits or on the occasional use of asphalted car parks is very much the province of the $\frac{1}{8}$th scale glowplug engined car. Contests divide into three classes of vehicle. There is Formula, which comprises cars following in miniature very much the same pattern as modern fullsize Grand Prix racing cars. Then comes Sports/GT again following fullsize practice, and, strangely enough the more popular of the two classes with higher speeds registered on account of their more suitable aerodynamic shape in a miniature size. Finally, and least popular, is saloon car racing, where the models once again follow fullsize racing practice, though not without some differences of opinion as to what is a saloon car. Except on very minor club 'fun' occasions it is not usual to mix the three classes in a single race.

Procedure at a meeting is to give some time for practice so that visiting drivers can learn the track, select their cut off points and generally get into form, like a knock-up before a tennis match. Then follows a series of timed heats are run, rather like the

Below: They come in all sizes! Quick reaction of youngsters driving cars well prepared by Dad will often leave the field standing! This is a shot by J-C Rumbeli of Switzerland.

Above: Mixed bag! Contestants at a friendly series held at Pontin's Holiday Village Model Week with both Formula and GT cars running together. Junior has slipped in his on the right.

fullsize struggle for grid positions before a Grand Prix. Where possible drivers are seeded so that less speedy cars will not impede known faster machines. This does not always work out with the form of visiting driver not completely known, though some idea can be gained from the first practice laps. Object of the heats is to get the fastest time over a short run of, usually, five minutes. Three separate heats are run and the drivers' best times are noted. The four fastest cars go straight into a final. Before this there is a sub-final where the next six fastest cars fight out the remaining two places in the final. It is not necessary to have won a heat to place in final or sub-final, time is the thing that matters. In England heats are normally for six cars, sub-finals and finals also for six cars. Overseas, where there is sometimes a wider range of permitted radio frequencies eight or ten car heats are quite normal. This is theoretically possible in Britain by using split frequencies to get up to a round dozen cars on the track at once, but this only happens during the less demanding practice running at the start of a meeting. During a race any interference of one transmitter with another could easily spoil the event and lead to an appeal for a re-run.

Sub-final and final will take place over fifteen minutes and half an hour, or sometimes even longer, which will demand pit stops to re-fuel since the small 4 oz (or 125 cc) fuel tanks will only run for a maximum of seven and half minutes at racing speeds. Some drivers manager to get a little more but not a significant amount. Pit work by the mechanics, as the cars draw into the pit lane to re-fuel is an important part of the race. Swift refuel by bulb-bottle which holds exactly the right amount may take only three to five seconds. With a lap at say twenty seconds it is easya to see that three stops for fuel at a minimum time can mean a gain of nearly half a lap — with hamfisted pitmen a contrary loss of valuable time. Other incidents may also influence a race such as stripping a tyre, damaging a servo or oiling up a glowplug. The driver impatiently stands on his rostrum while his man or men work on the car — sometimes leaping down to demand what the trouble is.

In addition to the main races of the day it is customary also to run a Handicap Final, which gives the less successful drivers a chance to run on even terms against the best. Handicaps are awarded on the known form of drivers. Initially all are classed as 'rabbits' and get the most advantageous handicapping. This takes the form of a zero handicap. Those with better form will have to beat the scratch men by increasing percentages as their skill increases and their handicap goes up. Thus a top driver might have a 40% handicap, meaning that he must finish 40% ahead of the scratch man to beat him. Very often new men go from scratch right through to top handicaps in little more than a racing season. Handicaps are adjusted immediately wins, or near wins are recorded. Next year's handicaps are published in the Association's Year Book, but are constantly being changed by wins or otherwise.

One of the important needs of any meeting is a good supply of track marshalls to put cars back on the track when they spin out, or right cars which have rolled over in an excessive burst of speed. This is provided by making it mandatory for the drivers in one heat to act as marshalls for the heat following. Volunteers are enrolled for the first heat of the day! Very important events may have marshalling done by the host club members and their sons and daughters but this is something of a rarity.

Starting procedures follow fullsize practice very closely. There is the exciting three-minute hooter calling cars down from the paddock when they can circle round a few times before the off, a two and one minute hooter, and the clerk of the course calling cars up to the start line. The starter, who is the winner of the previous heat, by custom, raises his flag and a count down of five follows. Mechanics who have been holding the cars raise their hands to show they are neither holding back nor pushing their cars and the cars crawl forward to go over the start line proper as the flag falls.

Recently, more affluent clubs have been following a 'Christmas Tree' starting pattern. Here a traffic signal type of post is erected in good view of drivers and mechanics. A red light gives warning for the mechanics to release followed by a green light for the off. A penalty follows any driver who jumps the start. The old starting flag is thus dispensed with, which seems rather a pity.

Other appropriate track flags are still used. There seems no special need for 'ambulance on course' but yellow flag to caution drivers to slow down for an incident ahead, plus black flag and number to call in a driver, and finally the famous chequered flag to indicate the end of the race are all in use.

A meeting such as has been described with the three classes of cars catered for, and with handicap finals as well may take place, at a push, over a Saturday and Sunday meeting, or more comfortably over a three day occasion when it is a public holiday

Below: A special occasion! Finalists for GT/Proto event at Lilford Park at the European Championship meeting. Mechanics crouch in front of cars, drivers stand behind. Left to right: Ronny Ton (Holland) Debbie Preston (GB) Peter Bervoets (Holland) Dave Martin (GB) — the winner, Peter De Carro (Sweden) Phil Greeno (GB).

Above: Friendly gathering of stock car enthusiasts for a meeting in Holland.

weekend. The BRCA clubs arrange a mutually acceptable programme each season so that the clubs all have a fair share of the dates, good, bad and indifferent. The leading clubs run their own 'big meeting' occasion each season and a number of lesser events. The main events all count championship points to enable drivers to be selected for their national team to compete in the European Championship. This event takes place in a different member country of EFRA each year. In 1977 France were the hosts at their magnificent miniature Paul Ricard circuit near Lyons. In 1978 the BRCA were hosts at Lilford Park, near Peterborough, which must be the 'Brands Hatch' of British model car racing. In 1979 Germany are hosts, and so on until all the member countries of the European federation have had their turn.

As to prizes, this is still happily an amateur sport. No cash awards are made but elegant trophies and awards in kind are presented to winners.

So much for glow plug engined $\frac{1}{8}$th cars in Britain, but this is by no means all. The Racing Calendar also takes into account the whole of Europe in arranging its programme. Each country may put on a national Grand Prix meeting in which any other member country can compete. This way drivers with time and cash to travel may get racing experience all over Europe, with something happening nearly every weekend. Every effort is made to see that these events do not clash, though this is sometimes inevitable and drivers must choose their meeting. It happened in 1978 when the Monaco World Cup meeting clashed with the British National Championships. Perhaps this was a good thing, for it enabled some comparatively unknown drivers to snatch the laurels from absent experts winning overseas.

Quite apart from calendar events clubs will run their own friendly meetings amongst themselves when racing takes place on a much less serious level.

Some clubs, such as the Mardave Owners' Club, operate on a price range system, that is a total price limit is placed on the cost of cars entered. This may take the form of class for cars costing up to £60, another for cars up to £90 and an unlimited class. Drivers may compete in higher classes at their discretion but not vice versa. This gives young drivers with limited pocket money a chance to race on equal terms machinery-wise and has proved quite successful within a small club, or neighbouring group of clubs. However, when drivers wish to take part in more ambitious events they often find themselves outclassed by more efficient cars.

Still keeping a glowplug engined cars, we have stock car racing, which again follows fullsize practice of grading cars according to skill and wins. Such grading is shown by

110

the colours painted on car hoods, ranging from white for beginners up through the colours to red for a top class man, and the very occasional super-champion with gold. Stock car racing also has a cost limitation that engines shall not exceed £35 and not be extensively reworked and that kits again be within agreed price limitations. Scratch builders must satisfy scrutineers that they have kept within limits, and can be called upon to produce replicas within the price limits.

Stock car racing is less of a race than a pursuit of laps. Cars circle and circle knocking off the laps and occasionally bumping another car, though, contrary to the belief of some, this is not the main object. Cars are robustly built within a formula, and do not have brakes. Circuits are a plain oval. It is therefore an excellent medium for youngsters without a great deal of pocket money, and for places where only a small amount of space — not much more than a school playground — is required. Once again there is lively interest overseas, notably in Holland where big entries and large attendances at meetings are normal. France, Belgium and Sweden have also taken stock car racing to their hearts.

The younger branch of 1/12th scale electric car racing has hardly had time in England to establish a main stream pattern of racing. In the USA it has been operating for several years, and the expectation is that Britain will adopt a modified version of the American rules. A large number of clubs are springing up. These range from the prestigious Ally Pally Electric Car Racing Club which races on the speed skating rink at Alexandra Palace in London down to the many small meetings held in village halls, school playgrounds and gymnasiums. A strong Midland group of clubs have organised inter-club and championship events. Other clubs operate a league table of regular matches with their members over a three-month season or longer. Sometimes points are awarded on a first, second, third, basis; or sometimes it is based on cumulative laps over the period. This latter system is rather unfair on the man who has the occasional off day.

Below: Cars galore! One of the occasions when as many as fifteen cars race simultaneously thanks to relaxation of waveband limits by a kindly Post Office. This was a team endurance event.

20: Contest Organisation

EVERY TIME you take a car out on the track, whether it be at your local club's fun weekend or an invitation from another club, a lot of people have put thought and hard work into providing what may seem a very simple little circuit. But is it that simple? Who came along early and swept off the leaves, arranged to borrow a lap recorder and some pit tables plus a loud hailer and rigged up that horrible canvas abortion that is to serve as the loo? Plus all the other necessary acts that must be done before a quite simple ordinary contest can be run.

It may be your task one day to organise a show of this sort and the club's reputation stands or falls on the excellence, or otherwise of the organisation. This then is an effort to show the necessary steps from start to finish of the organisation and running of an invitation event. According to its importance there will be more or less work involved, but, basically, the sequence of events and the things that must be done are the same.

Right at the start the club, or organisation must decide that it would like to run an event on such and such a date. Officials must then decide if the club strength is enough to provide the various people who will have days to play before and on the day. If figures look slim they may perhaps agree to work in conjunction with another local club for a combined effort.

Next step is to put up a date or dates for the BRCA secretary to slot into his Racing

Below: Contest spectacular! Many weeks of organisation and a skilled team of workers required to mount this World Cup event by the harbour at Monaco.

Above: Start of the Stock Car final at Worthing Fiesta meeting. Local publican provided area in his car park; local beauty queen presented prizes and smooth slick running plus a fine day ensured success.

Calendar. This means that the preliminary work for next year's meeting must begin towards the end of this season. Early birds tend to get the best dates, always allowing the importance or otherwise and the situation of your club circuit. It is a good idea to offer several alternative dates so that there is no question of 'referring back' from the BRCA. I assume of course that the club members belong to BRCA (or the Stock Car Association of course) and race under their rules.

With the date fixed and a programme agreed the real work starts. Perhaps we should digress for a moment and consider that programme. If a fully open meeting where championship points may be gained is desired then the pattern is fairly firm, there must be the three classes, sub finals and a handicap final worked in. For a one-day meeting this is an almost impossible schedule and so a regular Saturday/Sunday meeting is the thing. The less popular Saloon Class can be on Saturday, so that those who may have to work, or who don't run saloons, can still have a good date on the Sunday, with Formula in the morning, Sports/GT in the afternoon. However, less strenuous programmes can be considered such as a team race, a marathon, or a restricted class event. These would not necessarily be in the official programme, though it is helpful to have them mentioned; but there is less need to decide a long time in advance.

It is desirable, indeed essential, to have a contest committee formed who will share out the work between them and act under the control of a Clerk of the Course, Race Organiser or whatever title is decided the Chief Executive shall be given, The committee will get on with their appointed tasks, reporting back at regular intervals.

Here is a list of items needed to be done, decisions made, material obtained or work teams organised:

(1) Name, date, venue and type of event to be held.

(2) Nature of invitation to be sent out, price of entry, distribution of invitations, i.e. via Secretary of BRCA or how.

(3) Production of an official programme to sell to the public or just a simple duplicated sheet of rules, entries, etc.

(i) If to be sold, how much, what goes in it, advertisements to be canvassed for the club's profit.

113

Above: This is more the sort of trophy set that organisers should aim at. These are some of the awards to be won at the European Championship meeting.

Left: This massive trophy was awarded to Phil Greeno for his World Cup win. Nothing quite so splendid should normally be on offer.

(ii) Programme produced by outside firm who take the advert revenue but give the club either a round sum contribution or, more usually, a stock of programmes to sell for their own benefit. This saves a lot of club work if no member is strong in this direction.

(4) Press advertisement, posters for distribution in model shops likely to produce entries and any other publicity. A note to local press will often result in a few paragraphs on the news side and cost nothing.

(5) Sponsorship possibilities. Will any local firm of model shop be agreeable to assist financially or provide trophies or prizes in kind.

(6) Failing this, some idea of trophies to be costed, and bought bearing in mind probable revenue from entry fees which can be returned in prizes.

(7) With a possible shortfall of revenue, ideas for running a raffle or two on the day for say, an engine, a kit, or even a large can of fuel.

(8) Availability of suitable trestle tables for pits to be checked. If no cover in event of wet weather, hire of a pits tent or two.

(9) Possibility of power line to the circuit to enable entrants to charge up batteries, operate soldering irons.

Below left: Monitoring equipment made by Marconi (costing about £8,000!) Something a little more modest will suffice for most occasions. Below right: Camping facilities for tents and caravans should be provided for anything longer than a one-day meeting.

Above: The Leyton Raceway, London's own circuit. Possibly longest in regular use it is only a few miles from Central London. This shot from the rostrum shows about half of the circuit. Yet to run a major event.

(10) Public address system to be hired if not possessed by club. Loud hailer **could** substitute but not ideal.

(11) Stationery for the meeting, paper and boards to display entries and their times, heats etc. Self adhesive numbers for the cars.

(12) Armbands or other identification for entrants, officials, press etc, so that unauthorised people can be kept out of the way in the pits and paddock.

(13) Check state of drivers' rostrum, availability of course flags, starter's flag (Union Jack), black flag for bringing in a car, yellow cautionary, etc.

(14) 'Christmas Tree' starting lights if available.

(15) Arrangement for a suitable 'boffin' with test equipment to attend meeting to iron out any problems of frequency interference etc.

(16) Arrangement for a safe pound to hold entrants transmitters when not racing, plus suitable person/persons to manage the pound. (Wives or girlfriends very useful here.)

(17) Suitable people to do lap recording, and arrange some preliminary training for them: timekeepers ditto.

(18) Arrange for toilets. Not, please **not,** an old bit of sacking insecurely fixed round a hole in the ground. At the very least some sensible sort of latrine, perhaps made from a six foot length of open guttering mounted on trestles with a down slope to drain in deep hole. Plus a closed area with Elsan or similar bucket. Ladies should have at least two preferably three such buckets, decently private, plus a mirror and small table. Suitable notices directing would-be users to same (I never found the one at the Lyons European Championships; those who did say I was lucky!). More affluent clubs (Lilford Park for instance) have splendid caravan type loos with running water, washbasins etc . . .

(19) Arrange for refreshments. This can be done by the ladies if willing, or a local firm of caterers may be willing on a profit dividing basis — or for a flat figure.

(20) Arrange crowd barriers as necessary. Ordinary rope and stakes are adequate.

(21) Fix 3rd party insurance for the club. BRCA members are insured already but the club should also be covered as a group. Many local authorities or other owners leasing circuit or facilities will insist on this and state amount of cover required. Your local insurance man should be able to sort this out.

(22) Sundry tents (it is so often wet) for scrutineers, timers, other officials to be hired.

115

Above: Scene of the World Championship to be run at Geneva. Although a car park area it provides adequate running and spectator room. Land is too precious in Switzerland to make a purpose-built circuit a possibility.

(23) Course to be checked over for condition. Any necessary white lining to be re-done, odd puddle holes filled in and everything made spick and span.

(24) Car parking arrangements to be decided.

(25) Camping/Caravanning facilities arranged if possible.

(26) Local hotels to be checked for prices and availability within say a radius of ten miles, and booking facilities offered to entrants coming from afar.

(27) Arrangements for any contest dinner/banquet put in hand.

(28) A notable big wig invited to open the meeting by starting first race, or similar.

(29) Advise local Police, so that any necessary point control can be organised, and in any event is a courtesy so that unusual traffic in the area is accounted for.

Below: Lilford Park circuit situated in the country near Oundle and scene of some of the most exciting racing seen yet. In a country park and stately home it offers splendid camping and recreational facilities.

116

Above: Wombell Sporting Association circuit which lies in a heavily industrialised area but has been developed with the help of the local association to be one of the country's best tracks.

(30) Arrange for attendance of St. John's Ambulance Brigade/Red Cross or equivalent. There are always cut fingers, minor accidents, and faints likely at any meeting.

(31) Check working order of frequency peg board.

(32) Arrange for local model shop to have a stand at the contest to sell the inevitable odd item, glow plugs, fuel, etc, that entrants forget or run out of.

(33) Make direction signs and arrange erection.

This formidable list comprises most of the essential things — they may be others peculiar to a particular show or district that occur to organisers.

Then comes the organisation on the day. How many entries have been made? It is better to have pre-entry so that a time schedule can be plotted, but entry at the track can be permitted, perhaps for a higher entry fee, up to a total entry limit. In a popular district not too far away from the centre of things and with championship points at stake, then an entry of up to a hundred for the main classes can be anticipated.

Giving drivers three heats each of five minutes plus three minutes warm up time demands a minimum of 24 minutes per driver, assuming there are no dropouts from later heats from breakdowns, damage etc. Some slight delays may be expected between end of one and start of next heat, plus any radio interference to sort out, so add, say one minute per driver to make 25 minutes each. Divide this by six for number of cars in a heat and you have the running time of the preliminaries. For 100 drivers this amounts to almost seven hours. Then comes the sub-final and the handicap final plus the main final. These will be longer races, probably 15 minutes for sub-final and two half hour finals. Then a small period checking results and the prize giving, say $1\frac{1}{4}$ hours. This brings you to the finish time.

Some visitors may have far to go home, and work on the Monday so try to arrange finish not later than 5.30 pm. Finals **have** been run in gathering darkness but this is not the mark of a well run event. Prelims then with 100 take 7 hours ($3\frac{1}{2}$ hours for 50) so then add $1\frac{1}{4}$ hours for finals and prize giving and we have a days programme of $8\frac{1}{4}$

hours. If we then allow $\frac{1}{2}$ hour for lunch or other break and we should be starting at 8.15 am. This is quite a sensible time to start on the second day of the meeting when most people already on the spot (Many model aircraft meetings start at 6.0 am and I have known even earlier!). Saturday entry will certainly be lower if saloon car class is run, when 50 would be a very good turnout, and start can be as late as midday.

When running a team race a lot less time is needed, so that this can be arranged as a Saturday afternoon feature. Time should be provided to give all participants a good slice of practice time — 15 minutes should be aimed at as a minimum. Teams should normally be of not less than four nor more than six drivers; mechanics/pitmen can of course be drivers when not so occupied with the pitwork. Some suitable rule should make it mandatory for each car to do a certain minimum number of laps. Team events are normally run over a fixed time of say four or six hours, or can be for an agreed total of laps, one hundred, two hundred or whatever suits the timetable.

For some reason these events have not caught on in popularity as well as might be expected, but are a splendid way of enjoying a fairly carefree meeting, with a great deal of less serious activity, in fact more of a social occasion.

So far meetings discussed have all been aimed at the $\frac{1}{8}$th scale glowplug engined racing section. The growth of an electric 1/12th scale following running in quite different conditions means that this section too will soon be establishing a national Racing Calendar. This has not so far been arranged and clubs are making up fixtures on an informal basis. Many of the matters necessary for an open air meeting do not apply where an indoor meeting is to be run.

Left: Monaco circuit with its long, nearly 90 metre, straight and the tortuous chicane well protected by enormous 'Botts dots' to keep cars on the track.

Above: A good example of a circuit. Small 'Botts Dots' protect the hairpin bend. Boards retain cars from running into the pits. A raised rostrum takes care of the drivers. Pit tables in the shade of awnings (this is California) provide creature comfort. John Thorp runs this Pomona Speedway as an adjunct to his model shop and model manufacturing activities.

119

Above: Paul Ricard circuit near Lyons shows what can be done with the help of a generous sponsor who has built the circuit as a miniature of the full size Paul Ricard circuit used internationally.

It is quite practical to hold evening meetings at club level when an attendance of up to thirty-two members can easily work out a programme of ten or more races of five minutes duration running eight cars to a race by the use of split frequencies. Since electric cars require to be recharged at short intervals, a five minute race with a few minutes practice beforehand is a suitable length, though ten minutes would be the longest time practical at the moment. In between races, drivers of course re-charge their batteries, which takes twice as long as discharging (ie up to twenty minutes).

With the availability of indoor halls for short periods — school halls, drill halls, church halls and the like the evening mid-week meeting is most suitable for club meetings. Interest is maintained in the local scene by a League Table or other competitive arrangement that carries on from meeting to meeting. Less skilful drivers will also appreciate the occasional novelty evening, when efficiency manoeuvres are carried out against the clock with obstacles. One club has introduced caravan racing, when cars pull a model caravan. Here again skill contests, backing, turning and so on can be introduced.

Finally, in all spheres of r/c models, the Concours d'Elegance should not be forgotten. Many a car will never win a race but can win a concours. To avoid out and out 'showpieces' it is a wise rule that Concours winners must show their paces on the track for a minimum number of laps after the award ... this can sometimes be quite a hilarious conclusion!

APPENDICES

1: British Radio Car Association

THE BRCA was formed in 1972 following a meeting of interested people at the Aubrey Park Hotel in Redbourn, Nr Hemel Hempstead. Founder members at that meeting included such stalwarts as Keith Plested, Wes Raynor of Mardave, who put down the first purpose built circuit at Newbridge, Ted Longshaw, currently Chairman of EFRA, the European organisation, the Lindstroms who established the Yorkshire based Littlemore Park track, Dave Rogers, now masterminding electric car racing meetings at Alexandra Palace ... to mention but a few. There were many more and apologies at once for not including the names, tell me about it if you have been left out!

It can fairly claim to be the largest European organisation of its kind and a keen member of the fourteen country EFRA (Europaische Federation Radiogesteurter Automodelle) which manages national and international meetings, agrees compatible rules, and **tries** to avoid important date clashing. BRCA publishes a monthly newsheet *Circuit Chatter* which is basically national and international racing news and results, issues an annual handbook with racing and constructional rules, provides third party insurance in Great Britain for all member drivers and costs (1979) £4.00 a year to belong.

Below we give list of current officials (write to secretary Tom Martin to join) regional/area representatives, summary of current rules.

Association Membership

All applications for full membership and all general enquiries should be made to the Secretary, 7 The Green, Werrington, Peterborough PE4 6RT.

All applications for Associated membership (£2.00 per year) and Junior membership for under-16's (£2.00 per year) should be submitted to a Regional Representative for verification.

Association Officials

Chairman: K. G. Plested, PB Products, Downley Road, Havant, Hants. Tel Havant 471774. Evenings Emsworth 2607.

Secretary: T. H. Martin, 7 The Green, Werrington, Peterborough. PE4 6RT. Telephone (0733) 72114.

Vice Chairman: Paul Padgin, 100 Calverley Lane, Bramley, Leeds, LS13 1HE. Telephone (0532) 566603.

Assistant Secretary: 1/8th Tom Martin, as above.

Assistant Secretary: 1/12th Electric Mike Newman, 2 Western Place, Clayton Heights, Bradford, West Yorks.

National Handicapper: Jeff Lindstrom, 87 Ashwell Road, Bradford, West Yorks.

Editor Circuit Chatter: Brian De Boo, 18 Gresford Way, Wrexham, Clwyd.

Regional Committee Representatives

London/S.E.: C. E. Longshaw, 80 Pepys Road, New Cross, London. S.E. 14. Telephone 01 639 5080.

London N./H. Ctys: Phil Greeno, Phil Greeno Models Ltd, 9 Village Way East, Rayners Lane, Harrow, Middx. (Tel 01-866 7770).

Southern Region: Keith Plested, as above.

East: E. Brooker, Kennel Bungalow, Barnwell, Nr Cundle, Peterborough.

S. Midland: J. Elliott, 8 Jubilee Drive, Glenfield, Leicester. Telephone Leicester 874683.

W. Midland: R. Bates, 101 Vivian Road, Fenton, Stoke-on-Trent, Staffs.

N. Midland: D. Preston, The Spiral, Huntingdon Drive, The Park, Nottingham. Telephone (0602) 46665.

N.W./Wales. F. Livesey, 'Hilbre', 107 Station Road, Delamere, Cheshire. Telephone Sandiway 88 3888.

N. & N. Central Yorks: P. Pagdin, 100 Calverley Lane, Bramley, Leeds. LS13 1HE. Telephone (0532) 566603.

N.E./E. Yorks: A. Maulson, 1 Scrubwood Lane, Molescroft, Beverley, E. Yorks. Telephone Hull 882329.

S/Western: Richard Beckett, 9 Thornbury Road, Uphill, Weston-Super-Mare, Avon, BS23 4YE. Telephone WSM 26265.

2: EFRA—European Federation of Radio-Operated Automobiles

The B.R.C.A. is an affiliated member of E.F.R.A. Other affiliated countries are Austria, Belgium, France, Germany, Italy, Lichtenstein, Sweden, Switzerland, Spain, Yugoslavia, Holland, Luxemburg and Monaco.

President (1979): **TED LONGSHAW,** Beech Tree House, West Hill, Downe, Orpington, Kent.

National Association Addresses

Austria: *Secretary:* J. Maringer, Haunspergstr 21, A-5020 Salzburg.
Belgium: *Secretary:* Poussel Philippe, Rue Longue 168, 1150 Bruxelles. Tel: 02/731 1013. *President:* Denis Tassaux, Rue Emille Banning 52, Bruxelles. Tel: 02/648 7867.
Finland: *Secretary:* K. Kansakoski, Vahantuvantie 6821, 00390 Helsinki 39, Finland. *President:* Miniracing Litto, Box 7, SF 00401, Helsinki 40, Finland.
France: *Secretary:* Bernard Poupaert, 45 rue de la Capsulerie, 93170 Bagnolet. Tel: 857 1334. *President:* Patrick Rigot, 14 rue du Gal Leclerc, 94000 Creteil. Tel: 898 5241.
Germany: *Secretary:* Wolfgang Ribatsky, Lange Str 27A, 7901 Dornstadt, W. Germany. Tel: 0731/266312. *President:* Horst Griesel, Wetterstienstr 14, D8931 Wintermeitingen, W. Germany. Tel: 08232 3492.
GB: *Secretary:* Tom Martin, 7 The Green, Werrington, Peterborough. Tel: 0733 72114. *President:* Keith Plested, PB Products, Downley Road, Havant, Hampshire. Tel: 0705 47117.
Holland: *Secretary:* Gerard J. Hoogeveen, Franz Leharlaan 26, 2102 GP Heemstede, Holland. Tel: 023 267634. *President:* Peter Bervoets, Vyfherenstraat 48, Heemstede, Holland. Tel: 023 287851.
Ireland: *Secretary:* Matthew Evans, 12 Tullymore Park, Ballymena, Co. Antrim, Northern Ireland.
Italy: *Secretary:* Stanzani Guerrino, Via Sacconi 13, 51100 Pistoia, Italy. Tel: 0573/23771 366836. *President:* A.M.S.C.I., Via Carnavalli 68, 20158 Milano, Italy.
Lichtenstein: *Secretary:* Quaderer Erich, In Der Fina 16, FL-9494 Schaan. Tel: 075 25511. *President:* Bech Bruno, Immagass 7 FL)9490 Vaduz. Tel: 075 23932.
Luxembourg: *Secretary:* Noel Francis, 16 Dierwies, Echternach, Luxembourg.
Monaco: *Secretary:* Richard Lajoux, 19 rue de Millo, Monaco. Tel: (93) 301790. *President:* Daniel Noaro, 14 Ave de Fontvielle, Monaco.
Spain: *President:* Carlos Mersburger, Traversera De La Corts 198, Barcelona, Spain. Tel: 3308977.
Switzerland: *Secretary:* E. Bopp, Flurstr 30, CH-8302 Kloten. *President:* Leo Jost, Dorfstr 288 CH-8955 Oetwil a.d.l.
Sweden: *Secretary:* Siv Mosen, c/o SBF Box 4, S-12321 Farsta, Sweden. Tel: 08/930500 (day). *President:* Rolf Stahre, Flintbacken 12, S-64100 Katrineholm, Sweden. Tel: 0150-26204.
Yugoslavia: *President:* Avto Moto Drustov, Slovenija Avto, Sekcija Rcavtomobilov, 61000 Lbubljana.
Norway (to be approved): *President:* Per Erik Syvesstad, Maridalsvor 334 Oslo 8.

3: EFRA/BRCA Construction Dimensions

Formula

Wing: Max width 217 mm. Max chord 77 mm. Max height 140 mm. Side dams 102 mm long max. 77 mm high starting 13 mm above wing
Overall width: 267 mm max
Body width: 217 mm max
Canard fin width: 217 mm max
Tyres: Tread width 25 mm, 64 mm max. Min diameter, front 60 mm, rear 65 mm
Bumpers: Max bumper width 267 mm, front and rear. Front bumper must follow body contour.

Sports/GT/Proto

Tyres: Tread width 25 mm mini, 64 mm max. Min diameter front 60 mm, rear 65 mm
Overall width: 267 mm max
Body width: 267 mm max
Bumper width: May extend 7 mm beyond side of body, or to 267 mm, whichever is the lesser
Wing: Width 267 mm max. CHord 77 mm max
Spoilers: Max spoiler height 39 mm. Max spoiler length 51 mm
Dams: Max dam length 153 mm. Max dam height 39 mm. These dimensions can be exceeded if they are within 10% of scale
Note: Spoiler and dam dimensions include molded-in portions of body.

Saloon

Tyres-tread width: 25 mm min, 64 mm max. Min diameter 60 mm front, rear 65 mm
Overall width: 267 mm max
Body width: 267 mm max
Bumper width: May extend 7 mm beyond side of body, or to 267 mm whichever is less. May extend 13 mm forward of body and in same shape as body
Wing: All cars may run a wing with two options. (1) If a wing is used with the trailing edge 204 mm max behind the rear axle, then the max width must be 216 mm with a 77 mm chord. (2) If a wing is used with the trailing edge 153 mm max behind the rear axle, then the max width can be 267 mm wide with a 77 mm chord
Spoiler: A spoiler may be added to the rear of the body 39 mm high (including molded in spoiler) if a wing is not used. No side dams may be added.

FORMULA

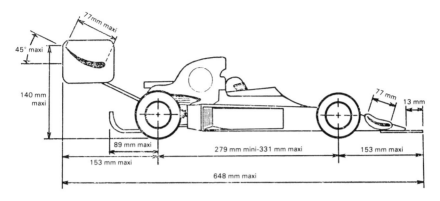

77mm maxi

45° maxi

140 mm maxi

89 mm maxi

153 mm maxi

279 mm mini-331 mm maxi

77 mm

13 mm

153 mm maxi

648 mm maxi

SPORTS/GT

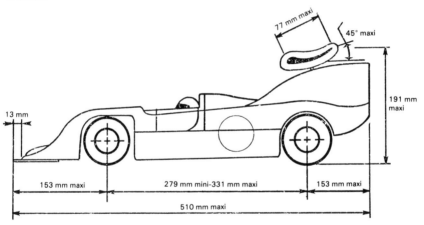

77 mm maxi

45° maxi

191 mm maxi

13 mm

153 mm maxi

279 mm mini-331 mm maxi

153 mm maxi

510 mm maxi

SALOON

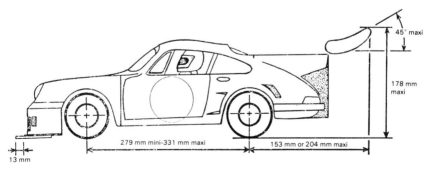

45° maxi

178 mm maxi

279 mm mini-331 mm maxi

153 mm or 204 mm maxi

13 mm

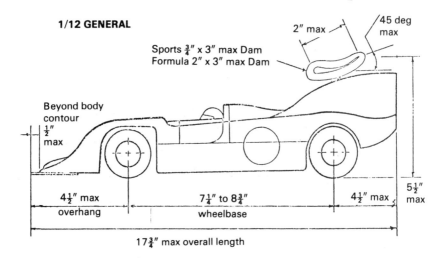

1/12 GENERAL

Sports ¾" x 3" max Dam
Formula 2" x 3" max Dam

2" max

45 deg max

Beyond body contour ½" max

4½" max overhang

7¼" to 8¾" wheelbase

4½" max

5½" max

17¾" max overall length

1/12 Electric Cars

1. All applicable ROAR general specifications apply (see drawing and dimensions below).

2. Radio — any legally licensed transmitter is allowed. Transmitters under 100 MW may be used at the operator's risk of interference from higher powered transmitters (When practical Race Directors should attempt to place under and over 100MW Tx in separate heat races. Comparison of times or scores will determine winners. In case of frequency conflict, fixed frequency loses).

3. Chassis — any chassis is legal provided it complies with general specifications.

4. Control — In addition to normal steering and forward speed control, operation in 'reverse' is recommended, but not mandatory.

5. Drive Motor — No rewound or modified motors allowed, including re-timed, balanced, epoxied or ball bearinged. Astro 05, Macbuchi RS54, Rowe-Mexico, Igarashi are allowed. Motor should be commercially available with a retail cost not to exceed (?) (This figure would have to be a matter of agreement, say, &10) Any new motors will have to be approved by rules committee (4 months?) prior to use.

This is USA list. European list to be published.

6. Nicad battery cells, nominally rated at 1.2 volts are considered the standard unit of battery power for electric car rules. Other types of batteries, if used, must not exceed the nominal voltage rating of their category.

7. Cars will compete in three categories:

(i) Production Class (unmodified) eligible to cars available to general public at least 90 days before the race. Motors must be out of the box unchanged (as per accepted list) but some latitude allowed in choice of wheels, tyres, axles and speed control. Ballbearings would only be permitted if part of the standard 90-day available car.

(ii) Stock Class anything ROAR legal in dimension and construction terms permitted, which means scratch built cars accepted. Restrictions; must be powered by approved motor (as per list).

(iii) Modified Class: Very nearly anything goes, reworked motors, epoxied, bushes, bearings, etc but stock armature and can must be used.

8. Race events should be of ample length (8 to 10 minutes) to further discourage motor modification. Batteries may not be **changed** during a race; though they can be **charged.**

General Specifications

Tyres: Tread width $\frac{1}{2}$ in minimum; $1\frac{1}{2}$ in maximum. Minimum diameter front $1\frac{3}{4}$ in, rear 2 in.

Overall width: $6\frac{3}{4}$ in maximum includes body, bumper, wing and wheels. Bumper: May extend $\frac{1}{4}$ in beyond side of body or to $6\frac{1}{4}$ in whichever is less. Wing: Width $6\frac{1}{4}$ in maximum Chord 2 in maximum. Spoilers: Maximum spoiler height 1 in Max length 1 in.

4: Clubs and Secretaries in the UK

ARRANGED by counties/regions, giving names of secretaries and showing some of the principal permanent race circuits.

Avon: Woodspring Radio Auto Club. *Secretary:* Richard Beckett, GB Models, 9 Thornbury Rd, Uphill, Weston-super-Mare.

Mendip, Brean, Weston-Super-Mare

A — Perimeter Fence — 3ft high
Infield Barriers — B — 1ft
Asphalt Surface
B
B
Pits
Drivers
Pits
Gate
Track: Length 675ft

Northavon Model Auto Club. *Secretary:* N. Bathe, 1 Homefield, Shortwood, Stroud, Glos. Tel: Nailsworth 2303.

East Anglia: Yareside Model Car Club. *Secretary:* Peter W. Robbens, Home Farmhouse, Home Farm, Somerleyton, Lowestoft NR32 5PR.

Bedfordshire: Chrysler Sports & Social Club (Model Car Section). *Secretary:* Barry Tingay, 24 Brampton Rise. Tel: Dunstable (604361).

Buckinghamshire: Aylesbury Electric Car Club. *Secretary:* Bill Burkinshaw, 14 Mowbray Rd. Tel: Aylesbury (21676).

Milton Keynes R/C Car Club. *Secretary:* Paul R. Burrell, 28 Caithness Court, Bletchley, Milton Keynes, MK3 7SS. Tel: 0908 - 647707.

Berkshire: Maidenhead Model Makers Club (R/C Cars Section). *Secretary:* Roy Price, Maidenhead Radio Models, 55 Queen St, Miadenhead. Tel: Maidenhead 37295.

Lilford Park, Oundle

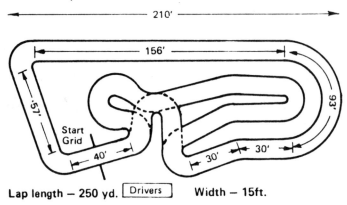

Lap length — 250 yd. Drivers   Width — 15ft.

Roarin' 20s Model Car Club: *Secretary:* C. J. Woolf, 7 Wheal Leisure Close, Perranporth, Cornwall, TR1 0EY.

Truro & District Model Car Club: *Secretary:* Dave Wellington, 9 Powhele Road, Truro, Cornwall, TR1 1RF.

Cambridgeshire: Lilford Park R/C Model Car Club. *Secretary:* Tom Martin, 7 The Green, Werrington, Peterborough, PE4 6RT. Tel: 0733-72114.

Wisbech R/C Model Car Club. *Secretary:* Wendy Mason (Mrs), 'Kyloe' 98 Sutton Rd, Wisbech, Cambs. PE13 5DR.

Clwyd: Rhyl & District Model Club (R/C Car Section). *Secretary:* Arthur Jones, 29 Ascot Drive, Rhyll, North Wales. LL18 2RW.

Wrexham & District Model Club (Model Car Section). *Secretary:* John K. Whittaker, 50 Herbert Jennings Ave, Acton Park, Wrexham.

Hoseley, Wrexham

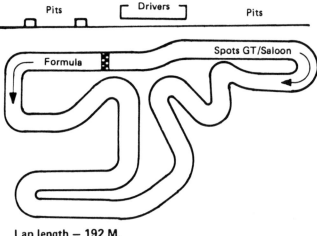

Lap length — 192 M.

Devonshire: East Devon Radio Control Club. *Secretary:* Ian Davies, Exmouth Models, Exeter Rd, Exmouth.

Torbay Radio Auto Club. *Secretary:* Bernard Portis, 23 Marldon Ave, Paignton, TQ3 3NY.

Derbyshire: Derby R/C Model Car Club. *Secretary:* G. M. Lowndes, 358 Sinfin Lane, Sinfin Moor Est, Derby DE2 9LT.

Tibshelf Radio Controlled Racing Car Club. *Secretary:* Ray Heffer, 24 Back Lane, Tibshelf, Derby. Tel: Tibshelf 2805.

Tibshelf, Derbyshire

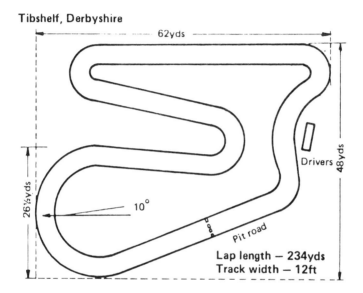

62yds

48yds

Drivers

26½yds

10°

Pit road

Lap length — 234yds
Track width — 12ft

Hampshire: Aldershot Model Club (Car Section). *Secretary:* G. A. Yarborough, Middle Watch, Glenville Gardens, Tower Rd, Hindhead, Surrey.

Firebird Model Club (Car Section). *Secretary:* John White, 29 Barton Drive, Hedge End, Southampton.

Portsmouth R/C Car Racers. *Secretary:* Keith Plested, 6 Record Road, Emsworth. Tel: Emsworth 2607.

Turbary Park, Bournemouth

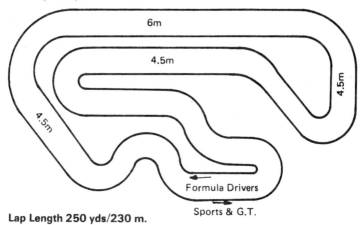

Lap Length 250 yds/230 m.

Hampshire: Tubary Common R/C Car Club. *Secretary:* H. W. Vear, J & H Models, 1288 Wimborne Rd, Northbourne, Bounemouth.

Skyryders Model Club (R/C Car Section): *Secretary (Cars):* J. Nicholls, 115 St Edmunds Walk, Wootton, I.O.W. Tel 883 120.

South Humberside: Scunthorpe Area Modellers Association (R/C Model Car Section). *Secretary:* J. W. Codd, 'Dunvegan' 94 Appleby Lane, Broughton, Nr Brigg, DN20 0AY.
Kent: Canterbury R/C Model Car Club. *Secretary:* Derek Smith, 7 Lenham Rd, Platts Heath, Lenham. ME17 2NX.

Gillingham R/C Car Club. *Secretary:* Gloria Hills (Mrs), c/o 51 Charter St, Gillingham. ME7 1NQ.
Leicestershire: Leicester R/C Car Club (Mardave Owners' Club). *Secretary:* Wes Raynor, 30 Roecliffe Rd, Woodhouse Eaves, Loughborough.

Midland Electric Radio Car Club. *Secretary:* George Godfrey, 174 Cedar Road, Earl Shilton, Leicester L9E 7HG.

Newbridge, Leicester

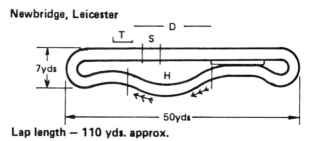

Lap length — 110 yds. approx.

Lincolnshire: Boston Radio Car Club: *Secretary:* M. Green, 59 Brand End Road, Butterwick, Nr Boston, Lincs.
Greater Manchester: Tameside Radio Control Model Car Club. *Secretary:* C. Whittaker, 4 Birks Ave, Waterhead, Oldham.
Merseyside: Liverpool Tigers Model Car Club. *Secretary:* George Whittle, 77 Blantyre Rd, Wavertree, Liverpool 17. Tel: 051-733 9460.

Wirral Model Car Club. *Secretary:* Mike Rimmer, 11 Norton Rd., West Kirby, Merseyside.

London

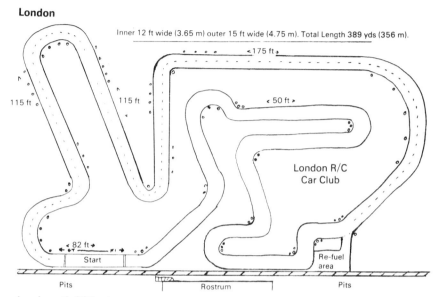

Inner 12 ft wide (3.65 m) outer 15 ft wide (4.75 m). Total Length **389 yds** (356 m).

London R/C Car Club

Lap Length 389 yds.

London: London Radio Car Club. *Secretary:* Bob Rosser, 17 Hapgood Close, Greenford, Middlesex. Tel: 01-864 7313.
South London Smoothies: *Secretary:* Richard Gammon, 46 Church Road, Barnes, SW13. Tel: 01-741 0333.

Middlesex: Ally Pally Electric Car Club. *Secretary:* Jane Adams, 79 Northumberland Rd, North Harrow, Middlesex. HA2 7RS. Tel: 01-866 5945.
West Midlands: Midland Electric Radio Car Club. *Secretary:* Tony Devenport, 200 Windmill Rd, Coventry. CV6 7BE.
Coventry R/C Model Car Club. *Secretary:* Bob Pulham, 387 Grangemouth Rd, Radford, Coventry. CV6 3FH. Tel: 596733.
B.R.D. Model Racing Car Club. *Secretary:* Keith Yates, 18 Braford Rd, Brownhills, Near Walsall, West Midlands.
Staffordshire: Stoke-on-Trent R/C Car Club. *Secretary:* J. W. Bossoms, 60 Duke St, Biddulph, Stoke on Trent. Tel: 514732.
Northamptonshire: Lounge Car Racing Club. *Secretary:* Tim Walden/Tony Wise, 10 Amberley Rd, Hartwell, Northants. Tel: Roade (0604) 863122.
The Paddock Electric Car Club. *Secretary:* Pete Bull, 12 Knights Court, Little Billing, Northampton.
Nottinghamshire: Nottingham R/C Car Club. *Secretary:* Dave Preston, The Spiral, Huntingdon Drive, Nottingham.

Oxon: The Gladiator Model Car Club (Oxford): *Secretary:* Alec Hudson, 2 York Close, Bicester, Oxon. Tel Bicester 45601.

Somerset: Taunton Radio Auto Club (TRAK). *Secretary:* Mike Lewis, 3 Longmead Close, Hoveland Park, Taunton. Tel: Taunton 85543.

Surrey: Chessington Radio Car Club. *Secretary:* George Dudman, 1 Chatsworth Gardens, New Malden. KT3 6DW.

Sussex: Eastbourne & District R/C Car Club. *Secretary:* Robin Lavender, 3 Hawkstown Gardens, Hailsham, Sussex. Tel: 841306.

Haywards Heath R/C Stock Car Club. *Secretary:* Pete Crawley, 16 Turners Mill Rd, Haywards Heath, Sussex. RH16 1NN. Tel: 533595.

Horam Model R/C Auto Club. 9 Tudor Walk, Framfield, Sussex. Tel: 618.

Southern Radio Car Club. *Secretary:* Peter Wooldridge, 6 Patricia Ave, Worthing, West Sussex. BN12 4NE.

Scotland: Aberdeen Radio Car Club. *Secretary:* Ray Cowie, 34 Thorngrove Ave, Aberdeen.

Clyde Model Car Club: *Secretary:* N. D. Whitfield, 69 Strathblane Road, Milngavie, Glasgow G62 8HH.

Strathclyde Model Auto Club: *Secretary:* John Wilkes, 73 Almond Road, Abronhill, Cumbernauld, Glasgow G67. Tel: Cumbernauld 31518.

Wiltshire: Swindon Electric Car Club: *Secretary:* Jan Korda, Swindon Model Centre, 2 Theatre Square, Swindon, Wilts. Tel: Swindon 26878.

Tyne & Wear: North East Radio Control Car Club: *Secretary:* J. W. Clark, 19 Oswald Terrace, Gateshead, Tyne & Wear NE8 1XU.

North East (Radio Control) Car Club. *Secretary:* J. W. Clark, 19 Oswald Terrace, Gateshead, Tyne & Wear. Tel: 771132.

Yorkshire: Beaverlac R/C Car Club. *Secretary:* A. Maulson, 1 Scrubwood Lane, Molescroft, Beverley, Yorks.

Keighley & District MES (Stock Car Section). *Secretary:* J. M. Varley, 10 Briarwood Ave, Riddlesden, Keighley, Yorks.

Wombwell Sporting Association (R/C Model Car Club). *Secretary:* Stephen White, 13 Derwent Drive, Chapeltown, Nr Sheffield. Tel: 62595.

Yorkshire R/C Model Racing Car Club. *Secretary:* Kenneth R. Hilton, 52 Bainfield, Liversedge, West Yorkshire. WF15 7PN. Tel: Heckmondwike 402690.

Rotherham Electric Car Club. *Secretary:* Phil Maxfield, 40 The Brow Brecks, Rotherham, S. Yorks.

Northern Ireland: Northern Ireland Radio Car Association. *Secretary:* Matthew Evans, 12 Tullymore Park, Ballymena, Co Antrim, NI.

Radio Stock Car Association

Chairman: Mark Bye, 63 Heathfield South, Twickenham, Middlesex. Tel 01-892-6634.

Secretary: Mike Varley, 10 Briarwood Avenue, Riddlesden, Keighley, Yorks.

Treasurer: Steve Talbot, Lectricar Racing, Rookery Lane, Groby, Leicester.

Press Officer: Linda Woodger, 1 Newton Close, Langley, Nr Slough, Berks.

Wombwell, South Yorks.

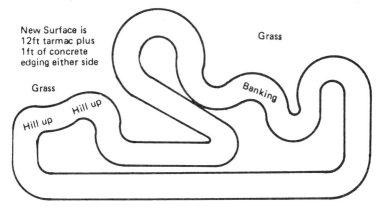

New Surface is
12ft tarmac plus
1ft of concrete
edging either side

Grass

Grass

Hill up

Hill up

Hill up

Banking

Lap Length 281yds.

Littlemore Park, Bradford

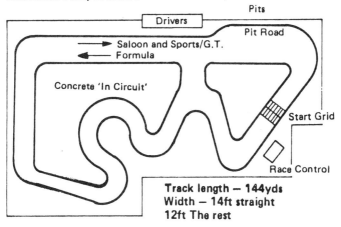

Drivers

Pits

Pit Road

Saloon and Sports/G.T.

Formula

Concrete 'In Circuit'

Start Grid

Race Control

Track length — 144yds
Width — 14ft straight
12ft The rest

Catfoss, Hull

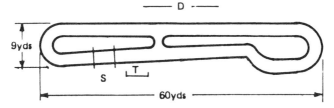

D

9yds

S

T

60yds

Lap length — 150 yd. approx.

133

5: Radio Stock Car Association Construction Rules

(1) **Scale:** Models are to be $\frac{1}{8}$ scale and a reasonable representation of an actual fullsize Stock Car.

(2) **Length:** Overall length to be within $16\frac{3}{4}$ in-$17\frac{3}{4}$ in.

(3) **Width:** Overall width to be a maximum of 9 in.

(4) **Wheelbase:** To be kept within a minimum of $11\frac{1}{2}$ in and a maximum of $12\frac{1}{2}$ in.

(5) **Bumpers:** Front and rear bumpers **must** be fitted with a contact surface of $\frac{1}{2}$ in-$\frac{3}{4}$ in and shall not project beyond the outer edge of the wheels. Centre line of the bumpers to be ground to be $1\frac{3}{4}$ in-$2\frac{1}{4}$ in.

All bumpers and nerf bars must be plugged and have no sharp edges.

(6) **Overriders:** These **must** be fitted to both the front and rear bumpers.

Front to be 1 in-$1\frac{3}{4}$ in high from the top of the bumper.

Rear to be a maximum of 1 in from the top of the bumper.

(7) **Nerf Bars:** These may be fitted to the chassis sides but **must** be on the same level as the bumpers and have a maximum contact surface of $\frac{1}{2}$ in but most not project beyond the outer edge of the wheels.

(8) **Tyres:** Width $1\frac{1}{4}$ in max.

Diameter $2\frac{3}{4}$ in min $3\frac{1}{4}$ in max.

(9) **Engine:** The maximum engine size permitted is 3.55 cc or 0.214 cu in. If more than one engine is used the total capacity must not exceed this limit.

(10) **Fuel Tank:** Size unlimited.

(11) **Silencer:** The engine **must** be effectively silenced to the satisfaction of the Race Organiser and be a maximum of 80dB at 10 metres.

(12) **Body:** The height of the body is limited to 4 ft-5 in measured from the top of the chassis.

(13) **Driver's Name:** This **must** be on the outside of the car.

(14) **Numbers:** All members' official association number **must** be shown on a 1 in high fin type number plate mounted on the car's roof facing sidewards. THe numbers are to be black and $\frac{3}{4}$ in high on a white background.

(15) **Grading:** Roofs **must** be painted in the drivers grade classification colour:

'A' Grade RED
'B' Grade BLUE
'C' Grade YELLOW
'D' Grade WHITE

All new members **must** paint their roof white.

RSCA Revised Grading System (Effective 1978)

1. Affiliated clubs, eg Coventry, Keighley, etc; to retain their own grading system, which will be honoured at all RSCA meetings.

2. RSCA members not belonging to a club, will be awarded points according to their placings *in consolations and finals only,* the actual number of points to be decided upon shortly.

3. Every two months, the points for each driver will be totalled, and roof colours allotted as follows . . .

TOP 20% RED
NEXT 40% BLUE
BOTTOM 40% YELLOW

Points are accumulated throughout the season

Drivers not gaining points will be white tops, and the 1978 season will start with drivers having end of '77 season roof colours.

4. Once a yellow roof is reached, a driver may not go to white again, even in subsequent seasons, (as at present). If gold top is reached, a driver may not go below blue.

5. It is impossible to assess the affectiveness of this system, except by trial, and alterations may need to be made during 1978. It is hoped that this system will create more blue and yellow tops.

6. Steve Talbot will be keeping a points total, and putting this system into operation during this season.

Cost Rules

Engine: The cost of the engine and carburettor must not exceed £35 at retail prices, including VAT current on 31st December, 1977. The only modifications permitted are those which can be carried out using hand tools, i.e., filing out exhaust ports.

Car: The cost of the car complete and ready to run, including body, heatsink and silencer, but excluding engine and radio equipment, must not exceed £35 at retail prices, including VAT current on 31st December, 1977.

In the case of scratch built cars the entrant must be prepared to produce replicas of the car, if so requested, for a price of not more than £30.

In the case of modified kit cars alternative modified parts may be fitted and the cost of the original standard part may be deducted from the total which must not exceed £30.

The entrant must be prepared to produce replica modified parts, if so requested unless they are commercial items currently available.

Procedure and Operating Rules: Every driver entering a RSCA approved meeting shall have proof of Association membership and a current GPO licence to operate radio control equipment.

Radios should have at least two frequencies available. Where frequencies conflict in finals, the fastest qualifier shall choose, providing it is possible for the other driver(s) to change to available frequencies.

The Race Organiser may request inspection of any entrant's car at any time to cover any or all applicable car specifications.

Any part of a car may be substituted during a meeting except the chassis.

6: Principal Manufacturers and Suppliers . . .

United Kingdom

Mardave R/C Racing, 30 Roecliffe Rd, Woodhouse Eaves, Loughborough, Leics. Kits, accessories, stock cars $\frac{1}{8}$th and 1/12th scale ic and electric racing. **Mardave.**

PB Products, Downley Rd, Havant, Hants. Kits, accessories, $\frac{1}{8}$th ic racing. Imports MRP 1/12th electric. **PB International etc.**

Lectricar Racing, Rookery Lane, Groby, Leicester. **Lectricar.** 1/12th scale electric.

B. T. Williams, 38 High St, Studley, Warks. **Puma.** Stock car kits $\frac{1}{8}$th scale ic.

Ke'Jon Kar, 243 Cheam Common Rd, Worcester Park, Surrey. **Ke'Jon.** Stock car kits $\frac{1}{8}$th scale ic.

Holland

FWF Engineering bv, Bakenessergeracht 21, Haarlem, Holland. Kits, accessories ⅛th scale ic. **Serpent.**

Italy

SG Racing Car, Via F. Albani 1-a, 40129 Bologna, Italy. Kits, accessories, ⅛th scale ic 1/12th scale electric and ic. **SG Futura.**
Mantua Model, Strada Statale 62, N.2/3/4, 46048 Lucia Di Roverbella, Italy. **Mantua.** Kits, accessories, ⅛th ic racing.
Turin's Model Car, Via Revello 55, 10129 Torino, Italy. Kits, accessories ⅛th scale racing. **Turin's Car.**

Switzerland

A. Steinmann Feinmechanik, Neue Winterhurerstrasse 77-79, 8304 Wallisellen, Switzerland. **Swiss Flash.** Kits, accessories ⅛th scale ic.

Sweden

Minicars Hobby AB, PO Box 464, S-75106 Uppsala, Sweden. **Challenger.** Kits ⅛th ic racing accessories.

West Germany

Johannes Graupner, Postfach 48, D-7312 Kiercheim-Teck, West Germany. Kits ⅛th ic racing 1/12th electric.
MFB Modell-Fahrzeug Bau GmbH, Herenpfad 26 Postfach 2141, D-4054 Nettetal 2. **Micart.** Kits ⅛th ic racing.
Modell Car Vertrieb, Nibelungenstr.81, D-6842 Burstadt. **Corsair.** Kits ⅛th ic racing. Accessories.

USA

Associated Electric, 1928 East Edinger, Santa Ana, Calif. 92705. **Associated RC.** Kits ⅛th ic racing 1/12th electric, accessories.
Bo-Link Industries, Box 80653, Atlanta, Georgia 30366. 1/12th electric.
Delta Mfg, Box 27 Lorimor, Ia. 50149. Kits ⅛th ic racing. Accessories.
Electrocraft Systems, 924 Fern Grove Drive, San Jose, Ca 95129. Kits 1/12th electric, accessories.
Leisure Electronics, 11 Deerspring, Irvine, Ca 92714. Kits 1/12th electric, accessories.
Dick McCoy/C & H Inc, 10767 Monte Vista Ave, Ontario, Ca 91761. Silencers, piston parts, engine mods, glo plugs.
JoMac (MRP) Model Racing Products, 12702 124th St, Kirkland Washington, 98033. Kits ⅛th ic racing 1/12th electric, accessories.
Parma International, 13927 Progress Parkway, Royalton, Ohio 44133. Lexan bodies ⅛th and 1/12th. Tyres, electric accessories.
Tatone Producrs, 1209 Geneva Avenue, San Francisco, Ca 94112. Silencers, radio plate, fillers, oddments chassis 1/12th electric and ic.
Thorp Manufacturing, 1655 East Mission Blvd, Pomona, Ca 91766. Miscellaneous accessories, differential, air cleaners, filler caps, carbs. (Owns Pomona pay track).
Ultimara Tyres, 8670 Chardon Rd, Kirkland, Oh. 44094. Tyres, wheels, starting gear, fuel.
Workrite R/C Hobby, 7009 Beaty Avenue, Ft Wayne, Ind 46809. 1/12th electric kits, parts.